A Colorado Kind of Christmas

Treasured Rocky Mountain Yuletide Traditions

Christmas is coming...

A Colorado Kind of Christmas

Treasured Rocky Mountain Yuletide Traditions

Collected and Edited by

LAURA McCLURE DIRKS

AND

SALLY HEWITT DANIEL

WESTCLIFFE PUBLISHERS, INC.
ENGLEWOOD, COLORADO

A portion of the proceeds from the mail order and phone sales of this book will benefit the Colorado Children's Chorale. To order additional copies, write or call:

A Colorado Kind of Christmas
Westcliffe Publishers, Inc.
P.O. Box 1261, Dept. CC
Englewood, Colorado 80150-1261

303-935-0900 in Colorado or 1-800-523-3692 from out of state.
(Please mention Colorado Children's Chorale when ordering.)

The Colorado Children's Chorale also offers *A Colorado Kind of Christmas* tape and CD. To place your order, please use the reply cards located in the back of the book.

International Standard Book Number: 1-56579-049-9
Library of Congress Catalogue Number: 93-060291

Published by Westcliffe Publishers, Englewood, Colorado
John Fielder, Publisher
Suzanne Venino, Managing Editor
Leslie L. Gerarden, Creative Director

Design by Rob Johnson, Wilson-Johnson Creative, Denver, Colorado
Nature photography by John Fielder
Christmas photography by Brian Litz (unless otherwise noted)
Food styling by Epicurean Catering, Denver, Colorado
Bonnie Beach, Copy Editor/Proofreader
Printed in Singapore by Tien Wah Press (Pte.), Ltd.

Reprinted with permission:
Music & lyrics for "Christmas in Colorado" by Samuel B. Lancaster
Descant for "Silent Night" by Duain Wolfe

Scripture verses are excerpted from the Holy Bible, King James Version

A Colorado Kind of Christmas is a trademark of Dirks & Daniel Companies.

Dedicated to:

The Candy House Kids

Katy

William

Anne

Katherine

Michael

J.T.

Ashley

Katy

Katie

Beth

Hewitt

and Aunt Fran

Welcome Home
to A Colorado Kind of Christmas

In 1989, we had both just turned forty, our children were growing up, and we had experienced the deaths of close, beloved family members. In short, we were each having a mid-life crisis! During the busiest time of the Christmas season, we found ourselves attending a very special Christmas program performed by the Colorado Children's Chorale. As sometimes happens, this performance was significant because it triggered thoughts about how we were living our lives and the legacies we were leaving our children.

Living in Colorado, as wonderful as it is, has separated both of us from relatives and loved ones. We come from different regions of the country—Laura from the Midwest, and Sally from the South. After having lived here for more than 20 years, we have adapted our own childhood Christmas traditions to the Colorado lifestyle. We came to realize that these holiday celebrations would form the basis for our children's traditions for the rest of their lives.

Christmas in Colorado means snow, skiing, sleigh rides, caroling, candlelit church services, or a trek into the forest to find just the right Christmas tree. How could we collectively save these experiences for ourselves, our children, and others? The idea for *A Colorado Kind of Christmas* was born from those discussions and from a determination to discover just what a "real" Colorado Christmas is.

As we talked about Christmas in Colorado and how it differed from the family traditions we grew up with, we realized that there were others in the same situation. Just like the pioneers of a century ago, many present-day Coloradans have moved here from other places, leaving behind family and friends in distant states. They, too, have tailored their holiday traditions to their new home. We wanted to portray our adopted state, its people, and their very special Christmas celebrations.

Our Christmas traditions are a blend of the past and the present, the result of our upbringings as well as the influences of living amid the snow-covered mountains of Colorado—the perfect holiday setting. In considering this, we began to see that traditions are formed through the repetition of family customs, and we wanted to examine our own Christmas traditions, as well as those of fellow Coloradans. We believe it is important to honor these traditions and pass them on—along with the stories of their origins—to our children.

Because a book like this needs to be based on fact, we began to research. We thought we knew quite a bit about Christmas in Colorado—but we didn't. After contacting every historical museum, chamber of commerce, resort association, and arts and humanities council that we could find, we then asked thousands of individuals to describe what "a Colorado kind of Christmas" meant to them. Their responses have been compiled in this collection, and we invite you to enjoy it and recall your own treasured memories and traditions as you celebrate the Christmas season.

Laura & Sally

P.S. If you would like to share memories, traditions or recipes with us, please write to "The Christmas Ladies" in care of Westcliffe Publishers.

Contents

Snow patterns of spring, Crested Butte

Fresh snow, Rabbit Ears Pass

Christmas in Colorado

Lyrics and music by Samuel B. Lancaster

Climb up to the top of Look-out Moun-tain and look out to the east at the lights of the cit-ies, twinkling like stars in a sky of fenced and fur-rowed fields. It's Christ-mas in Co - lo -ra -do. Then turn the oth-er way and look on mountains stretch-ing to the west. See the peaks of the Rockies, gi-ant snow stars top-ping waves of liv-ing Christ-mas trees. It's Christ-mas in Co -lo -ra - do. Christ-mas is the time when we long to have a star, our own star that will lead us on our

Sunset, Collegiate Peaks Wilderness

way   back to that child-like spot in our   hearts we'd for-got, where all we'd ev-er hoped for,

dreamed and   begged and prayed and longed for   waits to be   born.   So,

come and   climb with   me up   Look-out Moun-tain,   and   as   we   stand up   there,

lights spark-ling for us ev' - ry- where,   you'll find it's not too far to   grab a star   when it's

Christ-mas in Co-lo-ra-do.   It's   Christ - mas in   Co - lo -ra - do.

Editor's Note: "Christmas in Colorado," by Samuel B. Lancaster, was a gift to the
Colorado Children's Chorale.

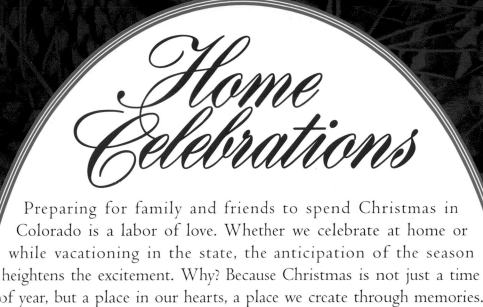

Home Celebrations

Preparing for family and friends to spend Christmas in Colorado is a labor of love. Whether we celebrate at home or while vacationing in the state, the anticipation of the season heightens the excitement. Why? Because Christmas is not just a time of year, but a place in our hearts, a place we create through memories. These cherished memories are brought out each year for reminiscing and celebrating anew. ❄ Home. The sights and smells of Christmases past and those yet to come help us realize the value of our own special traditions. Homes festooned with decorations remind us that Christmas is near. This is the time of year when we bring out the holly and the mistletoe. In Colorado we also decorate our very own Colorado blue spruce trees, both indoors and out. The smell of fresh evergreen permeates the house, a sure sign that Christmas is coming. ❄ Cookies bake in the oven, filling the house with the warmth of the season. The laughter of little children, trying to be extra good in case Santa is watching, adds to the holiday atmosphere. Ornaments—many handmade, others passed down through generations—are hung with care on the tree. The traditions of the season remind us that home is where we make it and that Christmas is a time of love.

A traditional celebration for Coloradans, as well as many others, is gathering around the fireplace to read The Night Before Christmas.

One of the most touching readings of this story takes place every year at the historic Hamill House in Georgetown.

During the weeks before Christmas, the local historical society celebrates with several evenings of dining and festivities. After dinner and caroling, children read the story aloud as part of the tree-lighting ceremony.

Written in 1822 by Clement C. Moore and originally titled The Visit of St. Nicholas, *the beloved story of Santa's magical visit is printed here in its entirety for your own holiday celebrations.*

*V*ictorian Christmas traditions are common throughout the state of Colorado. Many of these customs were imported directly from England, brought here by gold and silver barons during the mining booms of the late nineteenth and early twentieth centuries.

The legacy of our Victorian past, blended with the natural ruggedness of Colorado, brings a rustic elegance to the homes, decorations, and celebrations of Colorado Christmases. Most people envision the ideal Colorado Christmas as a cozy cabin nestled high in the mountains, surrounded by high peaks blanketed in snow. Inside, a blazing fire warms family and friends gathered round to roast chestnuts, sing carols, and toast the season with a traditional wassail. In this perfect setting, there are presents for everyone, our favorite foods…and someone else to do the dishes!

While reality may not necessarily match this picture, we nevertheless celebrate the holidays with family and friends and much-loved customs. Our home may not be the cozy cabin and there may not always be an abundance of presents, but we do have the mountains, the snow…and the dream of the perfect Christmas in Colorado.

*O*ur family tradition is to go to church on Christmas Eve, then have chicken soup for dinner and read The Night Before Christmas by the fire. Our edition was my Mom's and is from 1949.

— B.O'G., Littleton

❄ ❄ ❄

In hopes that

Saint Nicholas soon

would be there;

The children were

nestled all snug

in their beds,

While visions of

sugar-plums danced

through their heads;

Many personal accounts of how Coloradans celebrate their Christmases were shared with us. This story, taken from a diary, seemed to convey the special feelings and pride each family has in celebrating the season in their own way.

November 23

We had a really fun day decorating for Christmas. Denae, 4, wanted to wear her most recently acquired hand-me-down dress, a dark green calico trimmed with lace and velvet. First we walked to the mall to wave at Santa. Later, at home, we decorated a small tree with nativities cut from Christmas cards and glued in old jar lids. They were trimmed and hung with red ribbons.

We decorated our tree while "Come on Ring Those Bells" by Evie Carlson was playing. I had some blonde chocolate chip brownies ready to come out of the oven to eat when we finished decorating.

Denae taped Christmas cards on the door and put candles in an Advent wreath. She danced with Daddy in her beautiful dress to Christmas music, laughing and having a great time. We made a fun game of putting up the mistletoe, seeing who was going to get kissed. What a great time!

When David, 15 months, woke up from his nap, he noticed every new decoration. He filled our home and hearts with ooohhs and aaahhs as he pointed his chubby finger at each one.

—From the diary of Donna Burns, Littleton

The moon, on the

breast of the

new-fallen snow,

Gave a luster

of midday to

objects below;

Blonde Chocolate Chip Brownies

⅔ cup shortening
2¼ cups brown sugar
3 eggs
2¾ cups flour
2½ teaspoons baking powder

½ teaspoon salt
1 teaspoon vanilla
6 ounces chocolate chips
1 cup nuts (optional)

Cream shortening and brown sugar, then mix in the eggs. Stir in the remaining ingredients. Pat brownie mix into a greased 8½ x 11-inch pan. Bake at 350 degrees for 20 to 25 minutes. DO NOT over bake. Cut into bars before cooling completely. Makes 3 dozen.

Majeski Family Christmas

While in college, we could not afford many Christmas decorations or gifts, so we baked fruitcake using the old family recipe to give to friends and relatives.

In order to save the eggs to make into ornaments, we didn't break them. We made small pin pricks and blew out the insides, then we painted the eggs with lacquer.

That first Christmas we had one string of lights and 24 eggs on the tree. Through the years we have accumulated more lights, and the tradition of decorating eggs has persisted.

Using a variety of techniques, we now have 12 dozen eggs, which are the only ornaments we use. They have become our most prized Christmas possessions, and unpacking them each year is a very special part of our holiday season.

— Sue and Ken Majeski,
Denver

❅ ❅ ❅

When what to my

wondering eyes

should appear,

But a miniature

sleigh and eight

tiny reindeer,

With a little old

driver, so lively

and quick I knew

in a moment

it must be

Saint Nick.

*B*aking Christmas cookies is a memorable part of the holiday season. The aroma wafting through the house beckons you to the kitchen to snitch a few fresh from the oven.

Because Christmas is such a busy time, a "cookie exchange" is an ideal way to have a variety of homemade cookies on hand during the holidays. The concept is simple: throw a party and have each guest bring several dozen homemade cookies of her favorite recipe; when the guests have traded cookies with each other, they all go home with as many as ten to twelve different kinds of cookies!

Cyndi Duncan and Georgie Patrick of Greeley have perfected the art of the cookie exchange, which they describe in their cookbook, Colorado Cookie Collection. *Here are some of their suggestions.*

❄ ❄ ❄

More rapid than

eagles his coursers

they came, And he

whistled and

shouted and called

them by name:

HOW TO HOST A
Cookie Exchange

Planning:

With a friend, pick a date, time, and place. Then make a guest list. On your invitations indicate how many cookies guests should bring and instruct them to RSVP by sending their cookie recipe to the hostess.

Preparation:

Copy the recipes into a booklet for each guest to take home. Make name tags in several holiday patterns. Make two place cards for each cookie recipe, including the name of the cookie and the baker. Bake your own cookies.

On the day of the party, set up a refreshment area, including a tasting table, plates, napkins, and drinks—coffee, tea, or punch. Put one place card for each recipe next to a plate for each guest's sample cookies. In another room, prepare a cookie exchange buffet. It should include the second cookie place card and a box for each guest to use to collect the assorted cookies. If you have a large group, you may want to enlist two to four young helpers.

The Exchange:

Greet your guests at the door. Helpers take coats and hand out name tags and recipe booklets. Guests fill out address labels for invitations to next year's cookie exchange and are then directed to the refreshment area.

The helpers arrange six to twelve samples of each cookie on the tasting table. The remaining cookies are placed on the exchange buffet with the second identifying place card.

When all guests have arrived, the helpers select an assortment of cookies for each hostess and set them aside. The helpers stay at the exchange buffet to assist the guests. The hostess draws a name from the pre-addressed labels, and the group of guests whose name tags match the holiday pattern of the chosen name are invited to select cookies. Repeat this process until everyone has selected some cookies. Guests leave with a recipe booklet and a wide selection of cookies to enjoy throughout the Christmas season.

Cookie Exchange Favorites

Bizcochitos*
Cranberry Date Bars*
Eggnog Cookies*
Fudge Bill Likes!*
Gingerbread Boys*
Grandma Chrismer's Christmas Sugar Cookies
Kris Kringles*
Nana's Cookies*
Overnight Meringue Cookies*
White Fruit Cake*

*Check Recipe Index for these listings.

Grandma Chrismer's Christmas Sugar Cookies

My mother's recipe has been a favorite tradition in our family since I was a tot. For several years now I have carried this holiday tradition into Colorado by baking these cookies with my good friends, the Slavsky's, whose 3 children count on my arrival each December to bake and decorate hundreds of cookies.

Dough:
1 pound margarine
4 tablespoons sweet cream
1 pound powdered sugar
3 eggs
2-3 tablespoons lemon juice
1 teaspoon baking soda
5-6 cups flour

Frosting:
1 pound powdered sugar
¼ teaspoon salt
¼ cup milk
1 teaspoon vanilla
⅓ cup butter

Cream sugar and margarine. Dissolve the baking soda in lemon juice and add to the sugar and margarine mixture. Mix in the remaining ingredients, with the flour last, adding enough to stiffen the dough. Refrigerate for 1 to 2 hours or even overnight. Roll the dough out on a floured surface to about ¼ inch thickness and cut with your favorite cookie cutters. Bake at 350 degrees on an ungreased cookie sheet for approximately 8 minutes per batch, or until edges begin to brown slightly. Cool on a wire rack. Frost when completely cool.

To make the frosting, beat ingredients together with an electric mixer or food processor. Divide the frosting mixture and add food colorings as desired. Makes approximately 5 dozen.

— Dianne Chrismer

❄ ❄ ❄

'Now, Dasher!

now, Dancer!

now, Prancer

and Vixen!

On, Comet!

on, Cupid!

on, Donder

and Blitzen!

To the top of the

porch, to the top

of the wall!

Now, dash away,

dash away,

dash away all!'

Nana's Cookies

Sand tarts, pecan sandies, Russian Tea cakes…these cookies are called different things by many people. The recipes may vary slightly, but they all contain nuts and are covered with powdered sugar. This particular recipe has been a cherished family favorite for generations. — [Ed.]

1 cup butter
½ cup sugar
2 cups flour, sifted
2 teaspoons vanilla
1 tablespoon water
2 cups pecans, broken
powdered sugar for rolling

Cream butter and sugar. Mix in flour, vanilla, and water. Add pecans and roll into logs about 1½ inches long. Bake at 325 degrees for 25 minutes, or until the bottom edges just begin to brown. While the cookies are still hot and on the cookie sheet, sprinkle liberally and roll in powdered sugar. The heat will make the sugar stick. After cooling, pack between sheets of waxed paper in an air-tight container. Makes 3 dozen.

— Willie Mae Rogers

Eggnog Cookies

My sister, Becky, shared this recipe with me many years ago. My family likes the subtle eggnog flavor.

Cookies:
3 cups flour
¼ teaspoon salt
2 teaspoons nutmeg
1 cup margarine
¾ cup sugar
1 egg
2 teaspoons rum extract
2 teaspoons vanilla extract

Frosting:
⅓ cup margarine
2 teaspoons rum extract
1 teaspoon vanilla
2 cups powdered sugar
2 teaspoons cream or milk

Cream margarine and sugar; add flavorings and beat. Add remaining ingredients. Mix well. Form into logs or balls, then roll in sugar. Bake at 350 degrees for 15 to 18 minutes. Cool, then frost tops and dust with extra nutmeg. Makes 4 dozen.

— Susan Grupe

Kris Kringles

In early December we make hundreds of Scandinavian cookies, which we love to share with friends and family throughout the Christmas season. One family tradition is a "Kris Kringle" cookie which has been passed down from my grandmother.

1 cup shortening
½ cup sugar
2 egg yolks
2 tablespoons grated orange peel
2 teaspoons grated lemon peel
2 teaspoons lemon juice
2 cups flour
1 pinch salt
2 egg whites, slightly beaten
1 cup nuts, finely chopped
candied red and green cherries

Mix the first eight ingredients into a dough. Roll into small balls. Dip each ball in egg white, then nuts. Put a slice of cherry in center of each cookie and press down slightly. Bake at 325 degrees about 20 minutes, or until nuts are toasted. Makes 4 to 5 dozen.

— Karen Helling MacCarter

After baking our Christmas cookies and breads, we deliver them to friends and family.

— S.C., Evergreen

Our dream for a perfect Colorado Christmas would be to have all of our children and their families come home for Christmas!

—V.C., Burlington

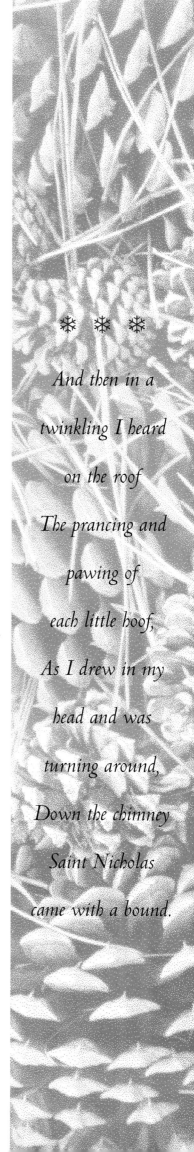

❆ ❆ ❆

And then in a twinkling I heard on the roof The prancing and pawing of each little hoof, As I drew in my head and was turning around, Down the chimney Saint Nicholas came with a bound.

23

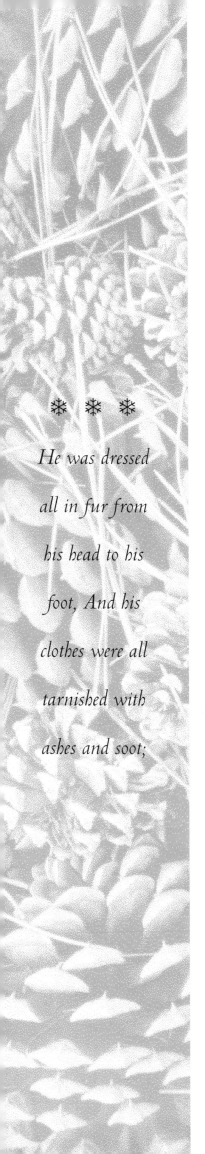

❄ ❄ ❄

He was dressed

all in fur from

his head to his

foot, And his

clothes were all

tarnished with

ashes and soot;

Fudge Bill Likes!

My son-in-law *loves* this fudge—so much that we named it for him!

4 cups sugar

1 12-ounce can evaporated milk

1 stick margarine or butter

1 pinch salt

1 cup semi-sweet chocolate chips

1¼ cups milk chocolate chips

1 7-ounce jar marshmallow creme

2 teaspoons vanilla

2 teaspoons rum

2 cups pecans, chopped

Butter a 3-quart oblong glass baking dish. Place sugar, milk, butter, and salt in a heavy pan on the burner. Turn heat to high and stir while cooking for 10 to 12 minutes or until soft ball stage is reached. It is better to test for soft ball stage, since a candy thermometer can be misleading at high altitudes.

Add chocolate chips and continue cooking until the chocolate is melted. Turn off heat and add marshmallow creme, pecans, and flavorings. Stir until candy begins to get stiff. Pour immediately into prepared pan. Place pan on a rack, not directly on the counter, and let stand overnight.

Cut fudge into small squares and keep in air-tight container with waxed paper between layers. Note: If you like peanut butter fudge, omit the pecans and add 1 cup of peanut butter when you add the marshmallow creme. Makes approximately 6 dozen pieces.

— Frances Ellen Hewitt

Overnight Meringue Cookies

Since these cookies are left overnight, it's great to put them in the oven just before going to bed.

2 egg whites
½ teaspoon cream of tartar
¾ cup sugar
1 6-ounce package mini chocolate, mint, or butterscotch chips
a few drops of food coloring (optional)
a few drops of extract to complement chips, such as rum,
    peppermint, vanilla, or almond
½ cup chopped nuts (optional)

Heat oven to 375 to 400 degrees for at least 15 minutes. Whip egg whites until soft peaks form. Add cream of tartar, sugar, food coloring, and flavoring. Fold in chips and nuts. Drop teaspoonfuls onto greased cookie sheets. Place in oven. Close door and turn off oven. DO NOT OPEN THE OVEN DOOR. Leave cookies in the oven overnight. Remove and store in sealed containers. Makes 2 dozen.

— Dianne Lindenmeyer

❄ ❄ ❄

A bundle of toys

he had flung

on his back,

And he looked like

a pedlar just

opening his pack.

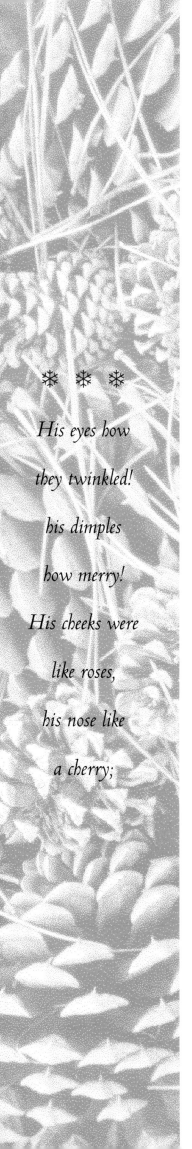

Gingerbread Treats

Gingerbread cookie ornaments are as much fun to make as they are to eat. This recipe combines several traditional versions and is especially good for "dunking." Little helpers can shape the clay-like dough, or the dough can be rolled out and cut with cookie cutters. Gingerbread men, Christmas trees, Santas, and stars are favorite shapes to decorate and personalize for cookie ornaments. For Golden Girl, pictured here, a gingerbread "dog bone" hangs on her family's tree to include her in the celebration.

Gingerbread Cookies

Dough:

½ cup butter	2½ cups flour
½ cup sugar	½ teaspoon salt
½ cup molasses	½ teaspoon soda
¼ cup water	¾ teaspoon ground ginger

Cream the butter and sugar. Add the molasses and water and mix well. Sift the remaining dry ingredients together and then add gradually to the molasses mixture. Roll the dough into a ball and chill in the refrigerator at least 2 hours.

Prepare the cookie sheet by lining it with aluminum foil. Then mix together ½ cup flour, ¼ cup sugar and 1 to 2 teaspoons cinnamon. Use this mixture to flour the rolling pin and surface. Roll out the cookies to ¼-inch thickness, thicker for larger cookie shapes. A straw makes a perfect hole for hanging if used before baking. Bake the cookies at 375 degrees for about 10 minutes. These may be enjoyed plain or iced. Makes 2½ dozen small cookies.

Icing:

1 tablespoon butter
1½ cup confectioners sugar
¼ cup canned skim milk

Mix the above ingredients. For a thicker consistency add more sugar. Use the icing to decorate your ginger bread cookies; add raisins or red hots for accent.

White Fruit Cake

This recipe is very old and originally had over two quarts of pecans in it. Over the years it has been cut in half twice and now makes one large loaf pan. It can be doubled to make a five-pound cake which fits in a round tube pan.

1 stick butter	½ pound candied cherries, chopped
1 cup sugar	½ pound candied pineapple, chopped
3 egg whites	½ cup apple juice
2 cups flour	1½ teaspoons pure vanilla extract
1 teaspoon baking powder	2 cups pecans, chopped

Cream together butter and sugar, then add the eggs. Sift together flour and baking powder, and mix into butter mixture. Add remaining ingredients. Bake at 300 degrees for about 2½ hours. Cook for less time if using small loaf pans. Place a pan of water on bottom rack of oven to help keep the cake moist while baking. Makes 1 loaf.

—Willie Mae Rogers

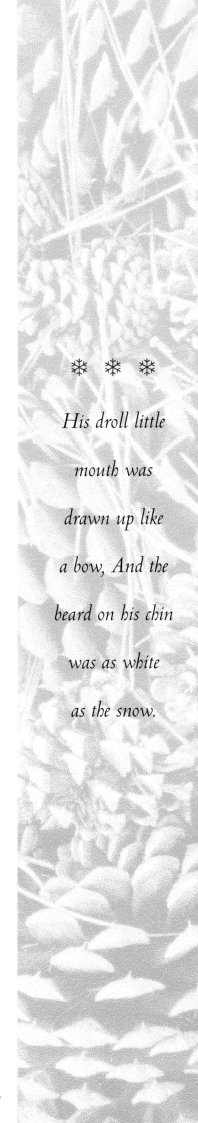

❄ ❄ ❄

His droll little mouth was drawn up like a bow, And the beard on his chin was as white as the snow.

In the early 1970s our family tradition of decorating candy houses was started by "Aunt Fran." From that beginning more than twenty years ago, this holiday event has now grown to include a dozen children as well as a few others slightly older!

We were delighted to learn that this Christmas tradition is also an annual custom for others, including the Eklund family from Vail.

To Make a Candy House:

Frosting:

3 pounds powdered sugar

9 egg whites

Beat sugar and egg whites for 20 minutes.

Suggestions for decorations:

candy canes—fences or doorways

red licorice twists—roof edges

chocolate candy bars—doors, windows, walk-ways

Life Savers—wreaths

striped gum—curtains, shutters

M & M's—walks, rocks, flowers

sugar ice cream cones—inverted for Christmas trees

marshmallows—snowmen, snowballs, snow forts

spearmint leaves—shrubs

chocolate cookies—roof shingles

shredded wheat—grass roof shingles

red hots

silver beads

colored sugar sprinkles

assorted hard candies

❈ ❈ ❈

The stump of a

pipe he held tight

in his teeth,

And the smoke it

encircled his head

like a wreath.

Things that make our Christmas special are the candlelight service at church, the Advent wreath, Christmas dinner, and making candy houses!
— K.D., Englewood

Eklund Family Candy House Party

One of our favorite Christmas traditions is to make candy houses with family and friends. We have a party where we serve hot glogg and apple cider, play Christmas music, and the children make candy houses.

Each child is given a cardboard frame for the house, a bowl of frosting, and a bowl of assorted candies. We tape the house frame to a round cardboard base saved from pizzas. The children then cover the houses with frosting and decorate them with candy.

It's fun to see how each individual child creates a holiday house. In addition to enjoying the finished candy house in your own home, they also make nice donations to raffles, hospitals, or needy families.

— Pelle and Chris Eklund, Vail

❄ ❄ ❄

He had a broad face, and a little round belly That shook, when he laughed, like a bowl full of jelly.

Skiing home, White River National Forest

A Crystal Farm Christmas typifies the dream many of us have of spending the holidays in the mountains with our families and friends. Getting ready for Christmas is a major undertaking and always more fun when lots of people help.

A Crystal Farm Christmas

Crystal Farm is the historic old ranch at Redstone Castle, in Redstone. It is nestled at the base of towering red cliffs that glisten with massive "icicles," just like nature's own Christmas spectacular. The farm is home to many who come here throughout the year and who gather together for the holiday festivities.

Each Thanksgiving all of the "adopted kids," considered "family" since their early college days in Boulder, gather at the farm. They make the trek into the mountains to find the perfect Christmas trees for the farm celebration. Not just any will do! One tree is for inside the house and the other is for outside. The outside tree seems to get progressively taller each year as the "kids" get older. Now they're not satisfied unless it reaches the peak of the two-story farmhouse!

This trek requires snowmobiles to get to the high mountain property owned by the family. After the trees are cut, everyone gathers in the cabin on top of the mountain for mulled wine and hot chocolate, huddling for warmth around the old cookstove before the long haul back down.

Then we begin the process of building a framework to hold the outside tree. The old backhoe raises it up, and we string the tree with lights. It all ends with a big Thanksgiving dinner to kick off the lighting of the tree.

The inside tree must wait, of course, until the weekend before Christmas when everyone gathers again to cut greens and make wreaths. The pine cones gathered on the mountain in the fall are made into decorations. Ornaments for the tree are handmade by a neighbor—an exquisite collection of porcelain-like angels created from Wonder bread and glue with intricate bouquets of flowers.

Christmas is for all family and friends who need a home away from home. They gather around the twelve-foot table that sits under the deer-antler chandelier, both made on the farm. Fires burn in the hearths of the old farmhouse. Over the main fireplace hangs a hand-carved wooden deer head wreathed in evergreens to celebrate the season.

— Joan Benson & Stephen Kent, Redstone

❄ ❄ ❄

He was chubby and plump, a right jolly old elf, And I laughed when I saw him, in spite of myself. A wink of his eye and a twist of his head Soon gave me to know I had nothing to dread.

*W*hile our homes are still decorated for the season and our friends and family are near, we like to toast the arrival of the new while remembering the past. The menu below is appropriate at any time during the holidays, but it's especially festive for ringing in the New Year. This buffet includes several delicious appetizers as well as sweets.

❋ ❋ ❋

He spoke not a word, but went straight to his work, And filled all the stockings; then turned with a jerk,

Open House Buffet

Asparagus Rolls*
Cinnamon Baked Brie
Chafing Dish Meatballs*
Olive Spread with Crackers
Teriyaki Chicken Skewers*
Spinach Mornay Dip
Shrimp Butter for Canapes*
Strawberries Dipped in Chocolate
Bourbon and Rum Balls

* Check Recipe Index for listing.

Asparagus Rolls

This recipe came from a friend named Ann. It has been and still is one of the all-time favorite appetizers that I serve.

Filling:
8 ounces cream cheese, softened
6 to 8 slices bacon, fried crisp
2 tablespoons mayonnaise
garlic powder to taste
⅓ cup pecans, finely chopped
2 green onions, minced

Other ingredients:
12 to 14 slices very fresh white bread
1 stick butter, melted
12 to 14 stalks fresh asparagus, steamed until very tender (Note: canned asparagus can be used when fresh are not in season.)
½ cup parmesan cheese, grated

Mix ingredients for the filling in food processor and set aside. Remove crusts from bread and roll with rolling pin until thin. Spread with filling and place one asparagus stalk inside. Roll up, cut into thirds at a diagonal, and place on baking sheet with seam side down. Brush with melted butter and sprinkle liberally with parmesan cheese. Bake in a 375-degree oven until light brown and crisp, about 20 minutes. Makes 36 to 42 bite-size pieces.

— Fran Strange

And laying his finger aside of his nose, And giving a nod, up the chimney he rose.

Shrimp Butter for Canapes

This may be used as a spread, to stuff cherry tomatoes, or as a filling in the asparagus roll recipe listed above. — [Ed.]

2 6½-ounce cans shrimp, washed and drained
¼ cup onion, grated
8 ounces cream cheese
¾ to 1 cup butter (no substitution)
4 heaping tablespoons Miracle Whip (no substitution)
3 tablespoons fresh lemon juice, to taste

Place all ingredients in food processor and mix.

Chafing Dish Meatballs

These meatballs do not need to be cooked before adding the sauce. They also freeze well. — [Ed.]

Meatballs:
2 pounds lean ground beef
1 package dry onion soup mix
3 eggs

Sauce:
12 ounces chili sauce
12 ounces bottled water
1 cup light brown sugar, packed loosely
1 cup sauerkraut, drained and finely chopped
1 16-ounce can whole cranberry sauce

Mix the ingredients for the meatballs and form into small, one-inch balls. Place in baking dish and set aside. Mix the sauce ingredients and place over low heat on the stove top. Simmer until bubbly, about 20 minutes. Pour over meatballs in baking dish. Bake in 350-degree oven for 45 minutes. Serve in chafing dish with cocktail toothpicks. Makes approximately 3 to 4 dozen meatballs.

— Libby Cottingham

Teriyaki Chicken Skewers

This teriyaki sauce can be used on chicken or beef. Everyone loves it! — [Ed.]

Marinade:
½ cup soy sauce
3 tablespoons honey
2 tablespoons vinegar
1½ teaspoons ginger

¼ cup salad oil
2 cloves garlic, crushed
4 green onions with tops, chopped

Pour marinade over 2 pounds of chicken cut into bite-size pieces and set in refrigerator overnight. Skewer and broil, 3 to 4 minutes each side. Makes approximately 20 cocktail skewers.

— Mary Jean Weigel

He sprang to his

sleigh, to his team

gave a whistle,

And away they

all flew like the

down of a thistle;

Christmas celebrations last through January 6th, or Twelfth Night, when the visit of the Magi is commemorated. In most parts of the country, Twelfth Night marks the traditional end of the Christmas season. Many Coloradans, however, consider the last day of the National Western Stock Show & Rodeo in January as the official end of the holiday season.

A Nancarrow Family Twelfth Night Celebration

Twelfth Night, January 6th, is a time for friends to gather and reflect on the events of the past year and to celebrate the prospects of the year ahead. The holiday is said to mark the arrival of the Magi in Bethlehem. On the liturgical calendar, it is an evening of merriment with a similar relationship to Epiphany that Fat Tuesday holds to Ash Wednesday.

Typically, Twelfth Night is an evening for adults and is a time to wear one's holiday finery—tuxedos and sequins are appropriate. Guests are asked to bring an hors d'oeuvre, a gift-wrapped Christmas tree ornament to exchange, and a small branch from their own Christmas tree, distinguished by a bit of ribbon.

When all the guests are assembled and the hors d'oeuvres consumed, the host invites all to partake of the wassail bowl, with one of the guests asked to propose a toast. A King and Queen of Twelfth Night are then selected through a random process to reign for the next several hours.

Paper crowns are bestowed on the royalty, seldom husband and wife, and all guests are required, thereafter, to do their bidding. The agenda for the rest of the evening is prompted by the host and hostess through the King and Queen. The first royal command is for the guests to be seated for dinner, which usually includes the following traditional menu items:

Turkey Chowder
(to symbolize the last use of the holiday bird)
Crusty French Bread
Spinach and Apple Salad
Tipsy Pudding
Wine and Coffee

Following dinner and dessert, the royal couple commands the guests to adjourn to the living room where entertainment is provided by either the guests, if previously asked to do so, or by the host and hostess. At some of our Twelfth Night celebrations, we have adopted a theme and planned the entertainment accordingly.

When the King and Queen have been entertained to their satisfaction, the guests all join in the singing of three or four Christmas carols. The evening draws to a close with each couple carrying the bough from their Christmas tree to the fireplace, sharing a New Year's wish, and then tossing the bough into the fire where it blazes brightly.

Twelfth Night concludes with the host or hostess offering a prayer for the whole group and the singing of Auld Lang Syne.

— Cliff & Debi Nancarrow, Gunnison

❆ ❆ ❆

But I heard him exclaim, ere he drove out of sight: 'Happy Christmas to all, and to all a good-night!'

Nordic skiing to Gothic, near Crested Butte

Family Celebrations

Family traditions are built around simple activities such as baking Christmas cookies, singing carols, trimming the tree, and entertaining family and friends. The secret ingredient in these gatherings is love, for no matter how old the children are or how far away family and friends may live, Christmas traditions transcend time and distance. True traditions radiate from the heart, beginning with simple events that are repeated in our families year after year. Over time, these events grow into customs and, in turn, become an expected part of our celebrations. ❋ Family takes on a special meaning in Colorado. In mountain resort towns, the Christmas holidays are one of the busiest seasons. Many of us are far away from relatives and loved ones, so people tend to band together, adopting friends as their new-found, extended family. In an effort to create a home away from home, they continue the time-honored customs of their childhood, merging old traditions with new. ❋ Family is an integral part of celebrating Christmas. Feasts are prepared, cherished toys and collections brought out, and memories of Santa's visits recalled. So whether our family members are related by blood, friendship, or simply by circumstance, we include our "family" in Christmas celebrations. For it is through family that we build traditions and pass them down from year to year.

Telluride Orphan's Christmas

Our tradition is the Annual Telluride Orphan's Christmas Eve Dinner. In Telluride, the majority of the people are far away from their families. And because the holidays are peak season in a ski resort town, it is difficult for most people to get enough time off to visit their families at Christmas.

The annual Telluride Orphan's Christmas Eve Dinner began in 1983. It's a very traditional event with a very traditional dinner. We have Christmas stockings and decorations, a big tree, and presents for everyone. Christmas music is played throughout the evening.

Dinner is usually served buffet style. It used to be a sit-down dinner, but now we are nearly 30 people! After dinner we hand out presents to everyone. Some leave around 11 p.m. to attend midnight mass at the local Catholic church.

On Christmas Day those who don't have to work go skiing, and we gather for a dinner of leftovers that night.

— Ruthann Russell, Telluride

Our family trims a live evergreen tree, and we invite someone who might otherwise be alone on Christmas Day.

— V.J., Ouray

We always try to invite others over who would otherwise be alone. It is a great way to have a bit of "family."

— P.D., Aurora

We neither one came to our marriage with any traditions, so we have developed our own over the past 28 years and our children have carried them on!

— J.K., Golden

A Creede Christmas for the Neffs

In the beginning of the century, around 1905 to 1929, a miner and his wife raised three sons in a log cabin above Creede. The miner worked his silver mine on the mountainside near his cabin while the sons hiked to school, or skied if it was winter, carrying snow shoes on their backs for the uphill hike home. They hunted and fished for their meat much of the time. Sometimes, they had trap lines to make extra money because the mother lode proved elusive to the miner. He never found it, but he did find a beautiful life high in the San Juan Mountains with his wife and sons.

Christmas was a special time for this family. They didn't have a lot of extras. Their cabin was simple with no electricity or running water, and it was heated by a woodburning stove. On Christmas Eve, the three boys went to bed as usual, with the cabin looking the same as it did on any day.

After the boys were asleep, the miner and his wife would go up on the mountain and chop down a fir tree and carry it back to the cabin. Sometimes this would be quite a chore because there might be a foot and a half of snow. The tree would have to be shaken out and dried.

While the boys slept, the couple decorated the tree with tinsel, glass balls, and little candles in tiny tin candle holders. Then they would set out the gifts by the tree.

There would be something for each boy, always sports or outdoor equipment, like a new hunting knife, fishing pole, or a baseball. One very special Christmas, there were two little trees, both decorated, with a pup tent strung up between and new skis crossed behind it.

Last, and most memorable of all, the miner, in the wee hours of Christmas morning, would go to the

Old cabin, San Juan Mountains

kitchen, fire up the stove and make crystal, snowy white Divinity Candy that he would roll out into a special sugary treat for Christmas Day. By the time everything was in place under the tree, it was sometimes almost morning; but it truly seemed to the boys that Santa had indeed come.

One of the boys who grew up with those beloved memories learned to make Divinity and became the candymaker for his family. Every Christmas he would make the same wonderful Divinity for his three daughters, who loved it and came to cherish it as their own Christmas tradition. His girls grew up and had families of their own and he made candy for his grandchildren.

Two years ago he died and Christmas wasn't the same without him. For the first time in a long, long time, there was no Divinity Candy at Christmastime.

Then last Christmas, one of the older grandsons brought an unexpected present to the homes of his mother and two aunts. He presented each one with a roll of the Divinity he had made, just like his grandfather's, just like his great grandfather's.

It was the best Christmas present ever!

— Alfred M. Neff, Creede
Beatrice Neff Trautman, Morrison

Our favorite traditions are to open one present on Christmas Eve, the rest on Christmas Day. We eat dinner in the living room by the tree, and we still leave cookies for Santa!

— A.D., Denver

The Neff Family's Divinity Candy

3 cups granulated sugar
½ cup light corn syrup
¾ cup water
1 teaspoon vanilla
½ teaspoon salt
¼ cup egg whites, approximately 2 eggs
1 cup chopped pecans (optional)

Combine sugar, corn syrup, and water in a sauce pan with a good fitting lid. Cook over low heat, stirring until sugar is dissolved. Increase heat and bring to a boil. Then cover and boil without stirring for three minutes. Uncover, insert candy thermometer, and cook evenly until thermometer reaches 265 degrees. In Denver use 250 degrees, and even lower at higher elevations. If you don't have a candy thermometer, cook mixture till it reaches hard ball stage. Remove from heat.

Add salt and vanilla to egg whites; whip by hand or with electric beater at high speed until stiff. Slowly beat in hot syrup, pouring a thin stream from a height of one foot above the egg whites. Continue beating until the mixture almost holds its shape, but is still glossy. This can be tested by allowing a small amount to run from a spoon into the bowl.

If desired, stir in nuts, then pour into a 6-inch square pan lined with waxed paper. Spread lightly into place. Cool and cut into 1½ inch squares. Makes 24 squares.

Try the following variations for something different:

Chocolate Divinity
Use the same recipe and stir in 3 ounces of unsweetened chocolate, melted and cooled, instead of nuts.

Peanut Butter Divinity Roll
Use the basic recipe, but beat until mixture just holds a peak. Place two strips of waxed paper on a board or table; spread a thin coating of butter on the paper and on a rolling pin. Spoon the candy in a ridge across the waxed paper, about 12 inches long and 2 to 3 inches wide. Roll with rolling pin to flatten out like pie dough, to a thickness of ⅛ to ¼ inch and about 20 inches square. Immediately spread ⅟₁₆ to ⅛ inch of peanut butter all over candy. Take hold of one edge of the waxed paper and pull it back over the candy to form a roll. Leave waxed paper on candy roll until cool, but not cold. Unwrap and cut into ½-inch slices with warm knife.

Christmas Eve is for family presents, Christmas Day is for Santa's presents.

— D.N.,
Manitou Springs

Children bring a sense of anticipation to Christmas. Many of us can remember the long days and never-ending nights just before Santa visits.

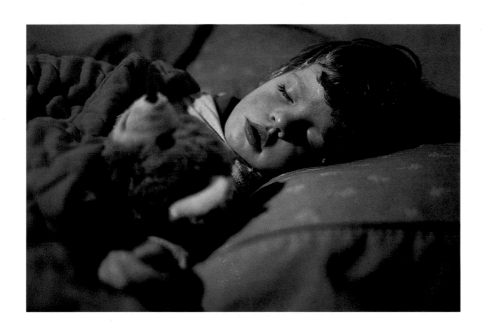

When my sisters and I were small we used to have great fun during the holidays. We would tie large leather straps with big bells on them around our waists. As we tore around the house we would sing our favorite Christmas carol, "Rudolph the Red Nosed Reindeer." We would get down on our hands and knees and gallop around, jingling merrily. It was so much fun!

— Shannon Kennedy, age 13, Englewood

Listening to special Christmas music, putting out cookies and milk for Santa and carrots for the reindeer, then going to sleep to wait for Santa.

— The H. Family, Westminster

Spending the holidays with our parents, and as many family members as possible. We eat macaronis—all kinds!

— R.R., Pueblo

Opening one present on Christmas Eve.

— S.W.P., Basalt

Looking forward to my grandmother's coffee cake on Christmas morning!

— S.V., Boulder

Singing carols while someone plays the piano or organ. The children tell what they liked about the last year.

— G.H., Aurora

Visiting old friends—or having old friends visit us!

— F.C., Parker

Spending Christmas Eve at Grandmother's house and Christmas Day at home.

— B.P., Englewood

Opening our gifts on Christmas morning, but we have a special husband and wife gift exchange on Christmas Eve after the children are asleep.

— C.J., Denver

Celebrating Christmas on the 24th and looking forward to midnight "mess."

— T.S., Littleton

Grand Lake Lodge Eggnog

This special recipe has been used for years to celebrate Christmas in August by the staff of the Grand Lake Lodge. I serve it in an antique hand-painted china punch bowl with a silver ladle.

12 eggs, separated
6 tablespoons sugar
2 pints whole milk
½ pint whipping cream
1 pint liquor (⅔ bourbon and ⅓ rum or brandy), optional

Beat yolks until lemon color. Add sugar, beating until dissolved. Add liquor slowly until eggs are "cooked." Whip egg whites until stiff; whip the cream separately. Add egg whites and cream alternately to yolk mixture to make a frothy beverage. Sprinkle fresh grated nutmeg on top. Makes 20 four-ounce servings.

— Bob Scott

Colorado Christmas Eve dinners reflect Victorian influences brought here during the late 1800s when the state was being settled. Roast beef was mentioned most frequently as an entree. This Christmas Eve menu tastefully expresses the varied foods and western flavor of the region.

Christmas Eve Dinner

Grand Lake Lodge Eggnog

Western Rib Roast*

Yorkshire Pudding

Horseradish Sauce

Colorado Layered Spinach Salad
with Pine Nuts

English Peas and Onions

Christmas Pudding*

* Check Recipe Index for listing.

Western Rib Roast

This western version of a beef roast will delight your family and guests! Tim Luksa, the executive chef at Epicurean Catering in Denver, graciously shares his secrets with us. — [Ed.]

1 15- to 18-pound western rib roast	2 tablespoons each black pepper,
1 tablespoon salt	granulated garlic, fresh rosemary,
	fresh thyme, and fresh marjoram

Trim fat cap from rib. Trim meat and fat up 2 inches from the end of the bone. Your butcher should do these first two tasks for you. Mix seasonings and rub all over the prime rib. Place in roasting pan and roast in preheated 275-degree oven for about 2½ hours. Remove from oven and let rest ½ hour. An internal temperature of 120 degrees will serve a medium rare, after resting out of the oven for 30 minutes. Increase internal temperature by 10 degrees for each level of doneness desired. Serves approximately 30.

— Tim Luksa

Christmas Pudding

This traditional "Figgy Pudding" came from my good friend Sue. We celebrate Christmas together, and this dessert is our families' favorite.

1 cup dried dates, chopped coarse	1½ cups flour
1 cup boiling water	2 tablespoons baking powder
1 egg	½ teaspoon baking soda
1 cup sugar	½ teaspoon salt
½ cup chopped nuts, pecans or walnuts	

Put dried dates and water in food processor and puree. Mix in egg, then add sugar and chopped nuts. Sift together flour, baking powder, baking soda, and salt. Add to liquid mixture. Place in a well-buttered mold and steam for about 1 hour and 15 minutes at 350 degrees. Test for doneness by touching to see if it is set. After it is done, invert onto an oven-safe pan and set aside. DO NOT DOUBLE THE RECIPE. Next make the vanilla sauce.

Vanilla Sauce:

2 sticks butter, melted	2 cups powdered sugar
2 eggs	1½ teaspoons vanilla

Melt butter in a heavy pan over low heat; add sugar and dissolve. Whisk in eggs, being careful they don't curdle. Cook till mixture thickens. Add vanilla last.

Warm pudding slightly if cool at serving time. Garnish with candied cherries or nut halves, then pour on vanilla sauce while it's hot. Pudding will soak up much of the sauce. Serve immediately. Serves 8 generously.

— Margaret Aarestad

We have two trees and have English "crackers" at each place for Christmas Eve dinner.

— M.W., Ouray

On Christmas Eve we gather at our parent's home to eat a large Italian meal and open gifts. On Christmas Day we return to eat a seafood dinner.

— J.B., Highlands Ranch

I like sitting around on Christmas Eve with the tree lit, candles lit and a fire in the fireplace. I like to talk and joke around with my family before going to bed.

— M.D., Denver

Our family spends Christmas Eve together. We tell stories about the family and then go to Mass.

— P.M., Edgewater

On Christmas Day, as families gather to open gifts, many celebrate with a festive breakfast. After an elaborate Christmas Eve dinner the night before, many families enjoy a breakfast or brunch in place of a big Christmas Day dinner. This Christmas breakfast menu features an outstanding apple cake.

Christmas Breakfast
Christmas Egg Strata
Grandma Hill's 3/4 Apple Cake
Fresh Pineapple and Strawberries
Orange Juice
Hot Spiced Tomato Juice*
Vanilla Flavored Coffee

* Check Recipe Index for listing.

Grandma Hill's 3/4 Apple Cake

I usually mix Jonathan and Granny Smith apples; Delicious apples are sweeter. It's wonderful with ice cream!

3 to 4 medium apples, sliced and peeled	¾ stick butter
Cinnamon and sugar	¾ teaspoon baking powder
¾ cup sugar	1 egg
¾ cup flour	⅛ teaspoon salt, optional

Slice the peeled apples into an 8x8-inch buttered pan. Sprinkle with cinnamon and sugar, stirring until all slices are covered. In a separate bowl, mix remaining ingredients; batter will be stiff. Spread it over the top of the apples so none of them are showing. Bake at 350 degrees for ½ to ¾ hour, until crust is golden and apples are bubbly. Serve hot or cold for breakfast, brunch, or dessert. Serves 6 to 8.

— Jan E. Kiefer

For variety, you may add ½ cup cold coffee, ½ cup chopped walnuts, and 1 cup chopped dates to create a moist cake with an interesting texture and flavor. Bake at 375 degrees for ¾ hour. — [Ed.]

Hot Spiced Tomato Juice

This recipe comes from an old friend and has been a favorite winter drink since 1968. Although I have lost touch with her, I think of her every time I drink a warm, soothing cup. Enjoy! — [Ed.]

4 cups tomato juice
2 tablespoons catsup
1 teaspoon salt, or less
⅛ teaspoon pepper
juice of one lemon and rind, grated
½ teaspoon Tabasco
1 tablespoon Worcestershire

Combine all ingredients and bring almost to a boil. Simmer for a few minutes to let flavors blend. Serves 6.

Our "extended" family makes our Christmas special. We always seem to have someone extra at our house. Mother finds gifts for everyone. She doesn't want anyone to be without a present to open on Christmas morning. We have a special breakfast and friends come by and visit all morning on Christmas Day. It is a wonderful day!

— K.H., Telluride

As a family gift, we always select a jigsaw puzzle to put together over the Christmas holidays. As the children got older, the puzzles became more difficult. This tradition started with my husband's family.

— N.L., Englewood

We have a big brunch after we open our gifts.

— G.S., Ft. Collins

On Christmas morning we open our gifts and call all of our out-of-state relatives on the telephone. It is everyone for himself for breakfast, but the main meal is at 1:00 p.m.

— P.D., Aurora

We invite the immediate family plus aunts, uncles, nieces, nephews, cousins, spouses, and grandchildren to congregate at one of our homes for a potluck dinner and to exchange handmade gifts. Each person gives one gift to one other family member. We draw names and set the dollar limit for next year's Christmas gift exchange.

— M.J., Denver

Tamales are our holiday tradition. Our entire family, more than three generations, enjoys making as well as eating them. Their preparation, however, is time consuming, but can be great fun if you have family and friends to help. It takes us about four hours.

— J.T., Denver

Many of our family members are from Colorado, Illinois, and Texas. We gather at the home that holds the most!

— N.I.L., Grand Lake

Christmas morning presents are followed by a big family breakfast of posole and green chili.

— J.Z., Denver

Being together, opening gifts, having a nice midday dinner with people dropping by makes our Christmas Day special.

— D.B., Westminster

Dinner on Christmas Day is truly a feast! Treasured family recipes are prepared and shared. Traditional favorites are roast turkey and baked ham with accompaniments galore. Both stuffing and dressing recipes compete with each other for space on the buffet table. Sweet potatoes and yams are also popular, though few can agree on which is best. The Christmas Day dinner menu listed below reflects a wide variety of Colorado favorites.

Christmas Day Dinner

Relish Tray

Toasted Pecans

Roast Turkey

Baked Ham

Apple Nut Sage Stuffing

Grandmother's Cornbread Dressing*

Sweet Potato Casserole

Mom's Yummy Yams*

Mashed Potatoes and Gravy

Fresh Green Beans

Cranberry Relish*

Cranberry Jello Salad*

Maureen's Snail Rolls*

Pecan Pie*

Pumpkin Pie

Cookie Plate

* Check Recipe Index for listing.

Apple Nut Sage Stuffing

Chef Jim Schlarbaum is chief of operations at Epicurean Catering in Denver. This is his personal recipe which he has generously shared with us. — [Ed.]

1 stick unsalted butter
1 large onion, medium diced
6 stalks celery, medium diced
2 Granny Smith apples, medium diced
2 cloves garlic, minced
1 teaspoon each fresh rosemary, thyme, marjoram and oregano
2 ounces fresh sage
1 teaspoon each fresh black pepper and salt
2 loaves fresh french bread, large cubes
1 pound walnuts, chopped
2 cups turkey stock
2 eggs

Saute vegetables, apples, and spices in butter until onions are transparent. Add to french bread and toss. Add walnuts, stock, and eggs. Mix well. Form into a mounded shape about 14x6 inches; refrigerate until cold. Make your stuffing one day ahead and don't worry if it looks too dry—it will absorb the turkey juices as it cooks. Serves 10 to 12.

— Jim Schlarbaum

*H*istorically many Coloradans have had to spend Christmas Day working. In the early days, people counted on the railroad to run, so for the railroaders, Christmas was just another day. Today, because peak ski season occurs during the holidays, transportation providers and ski resort, hotel, and restaurant employees must all work through the Christmas season. Ranchers, too, must tend to their duties on Christmas Day.

C Lazy U Ranch

A Meyring Kind of Christmas

Being a ranching family and living in rugged country here in North Park, our livestock must be tended every single day throughout the winter months, including Christmas Day. For this reason, our big celebration is on Christmas Eve, when the entire family and several neighbors get together for a delicious meal of prime rib, wild rice casserole, and a medley of vegetables.

After the meal, we all gather around a beautifully decorated tree, which we cut from our own property and decorate differently from year to year with various themes. The patriarch of the family, "Twist," who is now 84 years old, distributes the gifts from under the tree. Everyone is grateful and thankful for the goodness bestowed upon us for another year.

Christmas morning is "just another day," as our cattle have to be fed as always. The men feed and harness their teams of Percheron draft horses and set off on their sleds to feed the cattle. It's brisk and cold, steam rises from the sweating horses and the air sparkles with frost particles. It's truly great to be alive and to be doing what so many people can only dream of!

— Lucy Meyring, Walden

*G*athering at family member's homes for dinner and a gift exchange is how we celebrate Christmas.

— M.T., Fort Collins

North Platte River, North Park

Julia Tapia, a widow and parishioner at Our Lady of Guadalupe Church, has four children, ten grandchildren and two great-grandchildren. In 1944 she moved to Denver, where she raised her family. A story that she wrote for The Denver Post in December of 1986, reprinted here with permission, tells how she first came to know Santa Claus. Julia Tapia still makes empanadas for Christmas and still believes in Santa Claus.

Christmas Memories of Santa's First Visit

I don't remember doing much for Christmas until the year I turned seven. It was 1923 and we lived in Vaughn, a small town in New Mexico where children didn't know about things like Santa Claus. Spanish families had different customs in those times.

All that changed one evening in early December. My mother was cooking the evening meal over an old pot-bellied stove in our kitchen when my father came home from his job as a laborer for the railroad.

He changed into a freshly starched shirt and tugged on his familiar dark suspenders. Then, he joined us children at the kitchen table. There were five of us then: my brother Jake was 11, Frances was 9, I was 7, Mela was 5, and Emma was 3.

I remember my father's face that night. He looked tired from the day's work, but his eyes twinkled as if he had a secret he couldn't wait to tell.

After dinner, he got out the Montgomery Ward catalog that my mother used to order material for our clothes. But on this particular night, my father didn't look at cloth. Instead, he turned to the toy section and said we'd better put in our order to Santa Claus.

Well, we didn't even know who Santa Claus was! There was no radio or television in those days to tell children he would come on Christmas if they were good.

My father told us Santa Claus would come down the chimney of the stove on Christmas Eve and leave us presents. We were very happy about this idea. I remember how we all sat at the kitchen table looking at that catalog. We wanted to order everything, but my father laughed and told us to order just one thing each.

Oh, there were so many beautiful things to choose from! Jake wanted a play farm set, and Frances asked for a sewing kit because she liked to embroider. My two younger sisters wanted the same dolls.

But I saw this beautiful porcelain doll with jointed hands and curly brown hair. She even had green eyes made of real marbles that closed so she could sleep. I always wished I had light eyes like my mother's, which were hazel. But mine are dark brown. So, the minute I saw that doll, I knew I wanted her and nothing else.

My father wrote it all down in the letter, and we were so happy. My mother just smiled and shook her head; I don't think she knew much about Santa Claus either.

The weeks before Christmas, I wondered about this Santa Claus. Would he be able to read my father's writing? Would the stove be too hot for him to come down the chimney? Did he know I wanted the doll with the green eyes?

We keep a "Christmas Memories Book" where we write down special things about each Christmas.

— M.W., Ouray

We celebrate by opening packages on Christmas morning with family from Pueblo and New Mexico.

— S.L.D., Northglenn

54

Christmas Eve finally came and we had to keep our own traditions. Because Vaughn was so small, the priest only came once a month, so we couldn't go to Midnight Mass like we do now. But my mother sang "Noche de Paz," and we all joined her in singing "Silent Night" as we bundled up to go ask for *oremos*, an old custom where children go door to door singing in exchange for treats.

Later we made empanadas, stuffed pastries. My father would bring home the coal and the meat. In those days you didn't have oil so we had to use lard. My job was grinding the beef tongue for the filling.

After we finished, all the girls put on the new flannel nightgowns my mother had made us. We all slept in the same room in two double beds. We were so tired from the excitement, but we giggled and worried about whether Santa Claus would really come. We tried to stay awake and wait for him, but then morning came and we'd been sleeping and missed him.

We ran to the living room and saw that what my father told us was true: Santa had come in the night! And there was my beautiful doll!

When I think about my father and how he brought us Santa Claus, I feel so much love for him, just remembering these things and knowing how wonderful he tried to make our childhood.

— Julia Rael Tapia, Denver

Bizcochitos

Bizcochitos are traditional holiday cookies. I use a cookie press and make little Christmas trees.

6 cups flour, sifted
3 teaspoons baking powder
1 teaspoon salt
1 pound lard
½ cup sugar
2 teaspoons anise seed
2 eggs
¼ cup brandy
¼ cup sugar
1 tablespoon cinnamon

Preheat oven to 350 degrees. Sift flour, baking powder and salt. Separately, cream shortening with sugar and anise seeds. Beat eggs until light and fluffy; add to creamed mixture. If desired, add a few drops of food coloring to make red or green cookies. Combine brandy with flour mixture, using enough to form a stiff dough. Knead slightly, roll out to ¼-inch thickness, and cut with cookie cutters. Dust with the sugar and cinnamon mixture. Bake about 8 minutes. Makes 8 to 10 dozen.

— Julia Rael Tapia

The Colorado Children's Chorale

The spirit of Christmas is always apparent in the voices of children singing. A very special Christmas present given to the people of Colorado is the gift of holiday music performed by the Colorado Children's Chorale.

Norwest Bank Atrium

The Colorado Children's Chorale brings together two holiday favorites—music and children. More than 350 youths, age seven through thirteen, sing in the Chorale, known internationally for its talent, enthusiasm, and dedication.

Divided into five choirs that perform throughout the state during the course of the year, the Colorado Children's Chorale is in tremendous demand during the holidays. Their annual concert, "Christmas with the Children's Chorale," includes all the children and is a long-awaited event for many families throughout the region. The Chorale also appears with the Colorado Symphony Orchestra and Colorado Symphony Chorus in their annual Christmas concerts.

The children help light up the state by singing at the annual Norwest Tree Lighting Ceremony, taking place in the Norwest Bank Atrium in Denver, the Estes Park Community Performance at the Stanley Hotel, the Westminster Community Concert, and numerous other private and public celebrations.

State Captitol Building

*J*ust after Thanksgiving, the whole state lights up! From the Capitol in Denver to Burlington, Grand Junction, and Durango, buildings are illuminated. Lighting ceremonies often include parades and waving Santas. Everybody joins in as people decorate their houses, stringing lights along rooftops, in windows, and draping them on bushes and trees. The practice of outdoor Christmas lighting began in Colorado, as described in the following story.

Outdoor Lighting Originates with Denver Family

Community traditions often spring from a single episode or event, and this is true of the origin of outdoor Christmas lighting. In 1914, Denverite David Sturgeon, owner of Sturgeon Electric Company, wanted to make Christmas a little brighter for his extremely ill son. The boy, who was bedridden at the time, could not see the Christmas tree lights that decorated the family's living room. So the elder Sturgeon took some ordinary light bulbs, dipped them in green and red paint, and strung them up on a pine tree outside young David's bedroom window.

Pleased with his success, the next year Sturgeon decorated several trees in his yard, and many of the neighbors joined in to light up their yards as well. The neighborhood soon became the talk of the town, and people came from all over the city to enjoy the spectacle.

In 1918, the late Frances Wayne, a reporter for *The Denver Post*, began a newspaper campaign, supported by the Denver Electrical League, that blossomed into a contest for the city's best outdoor lighting. Denverites marveled at these displays.

The idea soon spread to include civic buildings. John Malpiede, former city electrician, took on the task of creating an elaborate outdoor display for the City and County Building at Denver's Civic Center. Sturgeon Electric Company acted as a consultant and contributed extensively to the city's displays. To this day Sturgeon Electric continues to lend support in a variety of ways.

— Elaine Hughes
President, Keep the Lights Foundation

*O*n Christmas Eve, we like to drive through the streets of our neighborhood to see the Christmas lights! We play Christmas music on the radio, then go home and have a late dinner. On Christmas morning we get up late and have champagne and orange juice while opening gifts. Then we call our families in other states.

— L.S., Aurora

*W*hat makes the holidays special? The Parade of Lights!!!

— S.A.J., Lakewood

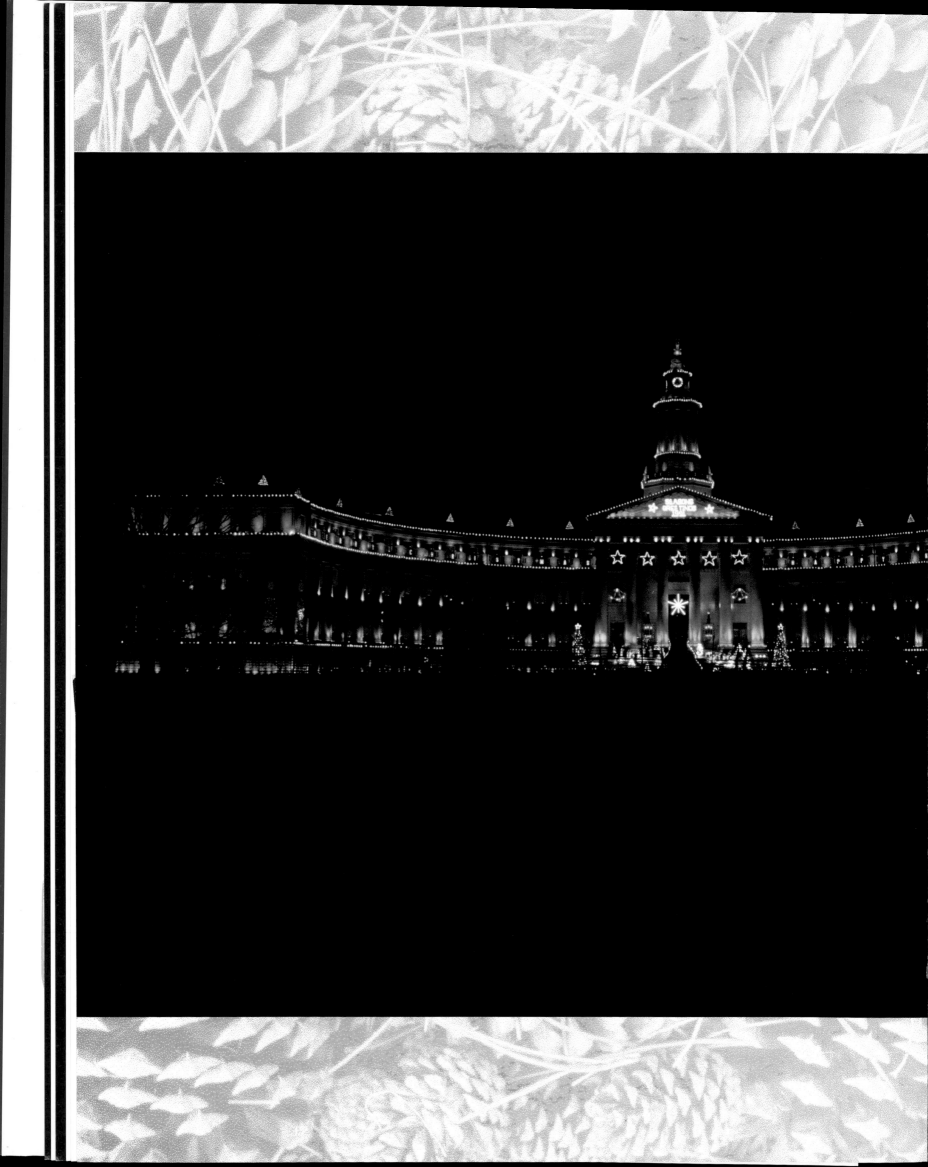

Denver City and County Building

The world's largest Christmas lighting display takes place in Denver from December 1st until after the National Western in January. Preceded by the News 4 Parade of Lights, more than 40,000 colored floodlights and bulbs are illuminated to decorate the City and County Building. For the lighting ceremony, Christmas carols are played in the ten-chime tower while thousands of people gather in front of the building and in nearby Civic Center Park to witness this spectacular display of lights.

The Keep the Lights Foundation raises money for the lighting of the City and County Building, a spectacular gift to Denver and the state of Colorado.

Our Christmas traditions include attending choir concerts, giving to the Angel Tree, caroling at a nursing home, driving around to see the lights and the Civic Center, family dinner on Christmas Day, and exchanging gifts.
— J.W., Denver

Castle Creek, near Aspen

Colorado Outdoors

You can find a picture-perfect Christmas setting right here in Colorado. It's the champagne snow, the sunny days, and the quiet serenity of star-filled nights! Mining brought adventurers to the state during the 1800s; today it's the snow and scenery that keeps us here and draws millions of visitors from around the world. ❄ Colorado boasts an average of 300 sunny days a year, but the nights—clear and crisp and sparkling—are what make winter special. It's not unusual to go to sleep with the snow just starting to fall and wake up to a bright powder day. That's the ultimate Colorado Christmas experience! Downhill skiers race to be first in the lift line, and cross-country skiers fill their backpacks with picnic lunches and head for the high country. ❄ As Coloradans we spend a great deal of time out-of-doors, and the holiday season is no exception. With friends and family we hike into the forest to cut Christmas trees, attend yule log festivals, and ride Santa trains with our children. And what's more festive than being snuggled under a blanket in a horse-drawn sleigh decorated with greenery, bows, and bells? ❄ To spend Christmas in Colorado, amid the spectacular scenery of the Rocky Mountains, is to truly feel the wonder and magic of the season.

*Torchlight parade
and fireworks, Aspen*

C Lazy U Ranch

Our favorite tradition is picking out and cutting down our tree from the hill behind our cabin. It's always a funny, odd-looking tree that needs to be thinned from the forest. When its decorated it's the most *beautiful Christmas tree!*
— B.B., Boulder

Dogsled trips through wilderness areas offer an exciting way to enjoy mountain scenery in winter. Some sled dogs, commonly referred to as Huskies, are hybrids of three original sled dog breeds—Malamute, Eskimo, and Siberian.

❄   ❄   ❄

Torchlight parades brighten the Christmas season with colorful nighttime displays at ski areas throughout the state. Carrying lighted flares, experienced skiers snake down the mountain in perfect formation with fireworks illuminating the slopes—a combination of Christmas, Fourth of July, and Mardi Gras.

Winding River Resort

The perfect Colorado Christmas would be a two-week retreat to a lodge outside Steamboat Springs with all the families of our brothers and sisters gathering to cross-country ski, snowshoe, and go on sleigh rides.
— The K.B. Family, Parker

Our ideal Colorado Christmas would be to stay in a wonderful, cozy mountain lodge and celebrate with a traditional Christmas dinner. We would ski, hike, sit around the fire and drink hot chocolate with the entire family.

— S.C., Colorado Springs

Covered Bridge, Vail

*C*olorado offers
some of the world's best
snow skiing, the result of a
dry climate and mountainous
terrain. Throughout winter,
downhill ski resorts and
nordic areas provide skiers
with thousands of vertical feet and miles of groomed trails. Some locations, such as
Vail and Steamboat Springs, even have bobsled runs.

Whatever your sport of choice, be it "shredding" the mountain on a snowboard or
leisurely cruising down blue runs, the time comes when the lifts close and the sun sinks
behind the mountain. After the day's strenuous activities, it's time to unbuckle your
boots and relax.

This is when friends gather to relive the events of the day, from that spectacular
mogul run to the faceplant worthy of movie stuntmen. Après ski activities are usually
casual affairs—meeting for a beer or cafe latte, gathering around a fondue pot, or
soaking in a hot tub. The natural mineral pools at Glenwood Springs are perfect for
après ski relaxation.

Snow angels inhabit Colorado!

The best ones appear when there is about eight inches of snow on the ground. To make a snow angel, you simply fall backwards into a pile of new-fallen snow. Then you flap your arms up and down and your legs open and closed. When you stand up, it will look as if an angel has left an imprint in the snow.

Reindeer

Christmastime is when children dream of Santa and his sleigh of eight tiny reindeer. While the animals are not common in the United States outside of Alaska, the largest herd in the lower 48 states is found in Colorado at the Flying Deer Ranch near Snowmass. Some of these reindeer pull sleighs in Denver's Parade of Lights. One wonders if reindeer really do head to the North Pole if given the chance.

My perfect Christmas? Lounging on a beach in Maui!

— C.D., Telluride

One of our Christmas traditions is to string popcorn and cranberries on the Christmas tree. We make extra strands to decorate the trees and bushes outside, which feeds the sparrows and squirrels.

— The J.O.K. Family, Aurora

We always begin our holiday season at the Parker County Christmas Parade.

— The K.B. Family, Parker

Colorado Cowboy Cookout

Colorado traditionally ends the holiday season with the National Western Stock Show. You can celebrate this annual event with a Cowboy Cookout featuring regional foods.

Colorado Lamb on a Spit
Pan Fried Trout*
Sage Camp Biscuits
Potato and Asparagus Skillet*
Apple Cinnamon Nut Cobbler*

* Check Recipe Index for listing.

Colorado lamb on a spit

*National Western
Stock Show & Rodeo*

Pan Fried Trout

Ice-fishing, a favorite Colorado winter sport, provides fabulous fresh trout for this recipe.

12 8- to 10-ounce trout, boneless	2 cups olive oil
salt, pepper and garlic powder	2 lemons
4 cups flour	

Season trout with salt, pepper, and garlic powder. Dredge trout in flour. Heat olive oil in iron skillet and fry trout until golden brown on both sides. Check for doneness by inserting a knife into the dorsal fin; fish will flake when done. Place trout on platter and squeeze lemon juice over it before serving. Serves 12.

Potato and Asparagus Skillet

This colorful dish could be a meal by itself! — [Ed.]

½ pound bacon, diced	2 red peppers, sliced thin
6 medium red potatoes,	1 bunch green onions, diced
diced into ½-inch cubes	2 teaspoons salt
2 pounds of asparagus,	1 tablespoon black pepper
cut into 1-inch pieces	1 tablespoon rosemary

Cook bacon in skillet until almost crisp. Add potatoes and cook until tender. Add remaining ingredients and cook another three minutes. Serves 10 to 12.

Apple Cinnamon Nut Cobbler

This recipe was developed to feed the crew of a cattle round-up. It makes a lot, but the recipe can be reduced to suit your needs.

4 7-ounce Martha White Apple	6 apples, sliced
Cinnamon muffin mixes	1 pound brown sugar
2 cups milk	8 ounces walnuts
2 sticks butter	

Preheat dutch oven in campfire. Combine muffin mix and milk. Slice apples. Remove dutch oven from fire and melt butter in pan. Layer apples, brown sugar, and walnuts. Pour muffin mix on top. Cover and place dutch oven back into fire and cover with coals. Bake 15 minutes, then remove and serve. If not cooked enough, place back in fire for a few minutes. Feeds 12 hungry cowboys.

The Cowboy Cookout and recipes were developed by Jim Schlarbaum, Director of Operations for Epicurean Catering in Denver, and Tim Luksa, Epicurean's Executive Chef. Both are avid sportsmen and acclaimed Colorado chefs.

We like to go to Winter Park, Steamboat, or Breckenridge for the holidays!

— S.L.D., Northglenn

My Christmas wish is to have all of my children and their families coming to spend the holidays in the Colorado mountains.

— L.W., Grand Junction

Durango & Silverton Narrow Gauge Railroad

Rio Grande Denver Ski Train

Santa's Winter Trains

In Colorado, Santa Claus has been known to use a ski lift, a snowmobile, skis, and even trains to make pre-Christmas visits. In Georgetown, Santa gives his reindeer a chance to graze while he rides the Santa's Express Train and listens to the wishes of young passengers.

For Lamar's Enchanted Forest, real pine trees come alive with the magic of Christmas. There is entertainment, decorated trees, visits to Santa's cabin, and miniature train rides for the children.

Since 1940, Coloradans and visitors have enjoyed the experience of riding the Rio Grande Ski Train. On weekend mornings during the ski season, the train makes a two-hour trip from historic Union Station in Denver to the base of Winter Park Resort. At the end of the day it makes the return trip with a trainload of tired skiers.

From Thanksgiving through December 31, excluding Christmas Eve and Christmas Day, the Durango & Silverton Narrow Gauge Railroad's Winter Holidays train chugs through mountainous snowscapes between Durango and Cascade Canyon. Originally built to transport gold and silver from the mines to the mills, this historic, coal-fired train now takes passengers on scenic sightseeing tours.

*N*ext year we would like
to rent a large cabin in
Glenwood Springs, ride
Amtrak up from
Denver, and bring along
family and friends to
just enjoy.

— D.F., Aurora

Georgetown
Loop
Railroad

Silent Night

Silent night, Holy night!

All is calm, All is bright.
'Round yon Virgin Mother and Child
Holy Infant so tender and mild
Sleep in heavenly peace,
Sleep in heavenly peace!

Silent night, Holy night!
Shepherds quake at the sight!
Glories stream from heaven afar,
Heavenly hosts sing Alleluia,
Christ, the Savior, is born!
Christ, the Savior, is born!

Silent night, Holy night!
Son of God, love's pure light
Radiant beams from Thy holy face,
With the dawn of Redeeming grace,
Jesus, Lord at Thy birth,
Jesus, Lord at Thy birth.

Star Peak, Elk Mountains

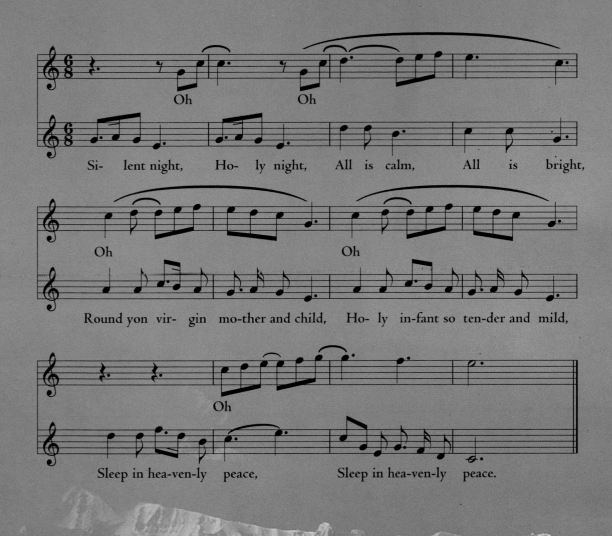

Oh Oh

Si- lent night, Ho- ly night, All is calm, All is bright,

Oh Oh

Round yon vir- gin mo-ther and child, Ho- ly in-fant so ten-der and mild,

Oh

Sleep in hea-ven-ly peace, Sleep in hea-ven-ly peace.

Lyrics and music by Franz Gruber, descant by Duain Wolfe

Sunrise above the Gore Range

The Christmas Story

When all the presents have been chosen and wrapped, the tree trimmed, and the holiday feast prepared, it's time to slow down and remember just what it is we are celebrating—the birth of Jesus Christ. ❋ Christmas Eve and Christmas Day are the most solemn—and the most joyous—of holidays. Cherished family traditions are based on how we celebrate these days, whether it be attending a candlelight service, singing Handel's *Messiah*, or reading the Christmas story from the Bible. ❋ Traditions differ depending on one's heritage, upbringing, and lifestyle. Some people host an open house on Christmas Eve and then attend a church service; some open presents at night, some on Christmas morning; some prepare a turkey feast, while others make empanadas. ❋ Everyone has their own way of observing the holidays, but a number of customs are common for all. We gather with family and friends, eat and drink, and enjoy each other's company. We exchange gifts and stories, using our time together to reflect on feelings and memories of days gone by. But perhaps the most common element of Christmas is that we all join together under the blessing of love, for it is truly a time for peace on earth and good will toward all.

Behold, a virgin shall conceive, and bear a son,
and shall call his name Immanuel.

— Isaiah 7:14

The Story of Christmas

And it came to pass in those days, that there went out
a decree from Caesar Augustus, that all the world
should be taxed.

(And this taxing was first made when Cyrenius
was governor of Syria.)

And all went to be taxed, every one into his own city.

And Joseph also went up from Galilee, out of the city
of Nazareth, into Judea, unto the city of David,
which is called Bethlehem, (because he was of
the house and lineage of David,)

To be taxed with Mary his espoused wife,
being great with child.

And so it was, that, while they were there, the days
were accomplished that she should be delivered.

And she brought forth her firstborn son, and wrapped
him in swaddling clothes, and laid him in a manger;
because there was no room for them in the inn.

— Luke 2:1-7

And there were in the same country shepherds
abiding in the field, keeping watch over their
flock by night.

And, lo, the angel of the Lord came upon them,
and the glory of the Lord shone round about them;
and they were sore afraid.

And the angel said unto them, Fear not: for,
behold, I bring you good tidings of great joy, which
shall be to all people.

For unto you is born this day in the city of David
a Saviour, which is Christ the Lord.

St. Aloysius Church, near Trinidad

And this shall be a sign unto you; Ye shall
find the babe wrapped in swaddling clothes,
lying in a manger.

And suddenly there was with the angel a
multitude of the heavenly host praising God,
and saying,

Glory to God in the highest, and on earth peace,
good will toward men.

— Luke 2:8-14

St. John's Church in the Wilderness

And it came to pass, as the angels were gone away from them into heaven, the shepherds said one to another, Let us now go even unto Bethlehem, and see this thing which is come to pass, which the Lord hath made known unto us.

And they came with haste, and found Mary and Joseph, and the babe lying in a manger.

And when they had seen it, they made known abroad the saying which was told them concerning this child.

And all they that heard it wondered at those things which were told them by the shepherds.

But Mary kept all these things, and pondered them in her heart.

And the shepherds returned, glorifying and praising God for all the things that they had heard and seen, as it was told unto them.

— Luke 2:15-20

For unto us a child is born, unto us a son is given: and the government shall be upon his shoulder: and his name shall be called Wonderful, Counselor, The mighty God, The everlasting Father, The Prince of Peace.

— Isaiah 9:6

Christmas Eve candlelight services are especially meaningful. While not all Christmas Eve services are candlelit, many Coloradans still list attending church on Christmas Eve and Christmas Day as the most significant part of their celebration. This seems to be true for all generations and denominations.

We asked people what it was about the Christmas season that made their celebrations particularly special. The following comments express some of their thoughts and feelings.

Ouray

Ryssby Church, Longmont

Simpich Character Dolls

We go to our Christmas Eve service, then come home and take turns opening our gifts while we eat snacks.

— L.K., Burlington

The Christmas Eve service at St. John's Cathedral is outstanding—the decorations, the tower bells, and the choirs.

— J.F.L., Englewood

Christmas Eve Eucharist with all the beautiful liturgy and organ music, choir, bell choir and singing congregation, are special to us.

— L.C., Greeley

We attend and participate in the local presentation of the Messiah.

— The M.F. Family, Steamboat Springs

Historic churches in
Lake City and Ouray

Moore Family Christmas

Our celebration includes family, neighbors, and others who live in our remote mountain town and who have no relatives nearby. We always host an open house after Christmas Eve church services. We serve finger foods and our version of English wassail, which is simmered from early afternoon until the party starts, filling the house with a rich, spicy smell. Since the gathering has become such a long-standing tradition, our guests often bring their own favorite Christmas goodies as well, so there is a wonderful spread. We usually have about 80 people, many of whom remain to sip wassail and visit until nearly midnight.

Coming together out of the snow and cold and celebrating the joy of Christmas with others reminds us of the true sharing aspect of Christmas.

— Charles, Penny, Travis, and Suzanne Moore, Silverton

Moore's Christmas Eve Wassail

3 12-ounce cans apple juice, frozen
1 12-ounce can lemonade, frozen
1 12-ounce can orange juice, frozen
1 12-ounce can pineapple juice, frozen

1½ teaspoons ground cloves
1 stick cinnamon
2 sliced oranges

Place all of the ingredients except the oranges in a large pot at midday and add enough water to make 2½ gallons of wassail. Wait a while and taste, adding ½ to ¾ cup sugar if necessary to sweeten. Simmer over low heat all day. One hour before serving add the sliced oranges. Makes about 50 six-ounce servings.

Blessing Bread

This is called "blessing bread" because it's meant to be given away— a "blessing" to others. It's extraordinarily good banana bread!

¾ cup shortening
⅓ cup vegetable oil
3 large eggs
1½ cups brown sugar
¾ cup white sugar
1 cup bananas, mashed
½ cup chopped nuts (optional)

1 teaspoon vanilla
1 teaspoon baking soda
1 teaspoon baking powder
¾ teaspoon cinnamon
1½ cups zucchini, grated
2½ cups flour

Mix first five ingredients. When the sugars and oil are well creamed, add bananas and vanilla. Mix well. Blend in baking soda, powder, and cinnamon. When all is blended, mix in zucchini, flour, and nuts. Grease and flour 3 loaf pans and line the bottoms with waxed paper. Bake at 350 degrees for 55 to 60 minutes. Makes 3 loaves.

— Lynn Cave

. . .and lo, the star, which they saw in the east, went before them, till it came and stood over where the young child was.

When they saw the star, they rejoiced with exceeding great joy.

And when they were come into the house, they saw the young child with Mary his mother, and fell down, and worshipped him: and when they had opened their treasures, they presented unto him gifts; gold, and frankincense, and myrrh.

And being warned of God in a dream that they should not return to Herod, they departed into their own country another way.

— Matthew 2:9-12

Cooper Family Christmas

Our family Christmas tradition was going back to my grandparent's farm. We always hung icicles on the tree for there was no snow in the south! I remember lots and lots of presents—not expensive ones but each wrapped separately and opened Christmas morning.

My husband grew up in Argentina, where Christmas is in the middle of summer. Gifts were not given in Argentina on Christmas, but on January 6th children set their shoes outside the door and a present was found in them the next morning.

Simpich Character Dolls

Now, as then, we open presents after eating breakfast and reading the Christmas story from the Bible. Adapting to our American tradition was an adjustment for my husband. He has now, however, discovered the wonderful joy of gift giving.

— Jean Cooper, Littleton

We open one gift Christmas Eve around the tree, then we wake up early to open gifts and see what Santa left during the night. Then we have a huge Christmas dinner with the whole family, or as many as can make it.

— P.M., Denver

When the children were younger, they acted out the Christmas story using the Nativity characters and then we opened our gifts.

— C.M., Englewood

On December 24 we open the gifts and set up nativities from all over the world. I have collected 55 sets.

— R.H., Colorado Springs

Cornice at sunrise, Oh-Be-Joyful Wilderness

Bev and Jay Labe
Todd Lampe
Samuel B. Lancaster
Michael Lane
Charlotte Lauric
Nancy Lavington
Don and Karen Sue
    Lawhead
Addie Lawrence
Fred and Nellie Lawrence
Bill Lee
Sarah Leffen
Parker Lenure
Kay Lenure
Nicole Leshaw
Betty R. Lewis-Labe
Gene and Maureen
    Lienert
Steve and Marilyn
    Lindenbaum
Dianne Lindenmeyer
Barbara Loken
Monique Lopez
Vivian Lowe
Helen Lowrey
Lt. April L. Lubliner
Bill Luetzen
Timothy P. Luksa
Tom Lundell
W. Thomas Lundell
John Luzader
Daryl and Karen
    MacCarter
Dan MacEachen
Megan Mackenzie
Joan Maclachlan
Ken and Sue Majeski
Stefan Majeski
Jody Maliga-LeJeune and
    Family
Cheryl Malina
Dustin Malina
Paula Manini
Kerry Manion
Mark Mantzke
Pauline Marshall
Tom and Cydney
    Marsico
Julie Martin
Elizabeth Marvin
Kristina Maxfield
Gail McBride
Louis McBurney
Jody McCabe
Molly McCarthy
Patti McCarthy

Elizabeth McCarthy
Chris McCauley
Michael McClure
Therese McClure
Nicole McGown
Leslie McKay
Ed McKeever
Michael N. McKenna
Christina A. McLean
Pat McMullin
Mardi McTeer
Carol Meisenheimer
Ken Meredith Family
Ann Hatfield Merritt
Ed and Kay Messenger
Judith Metcalfe
Richard Metzski
Lucy Meyring
Ralph and Peggy Miller
Mary Kay Mitchell
Posey Moller
Mike and Janice Moore
Charles, Penny, Travis,
    and Suzanne Moore
Loretta Morgan
Shirley Morrison
John and Jean Moseley
    Family
Sally Mundell
Barbara L. Muntyan
David Murphy
Susan Murray
Cliff and Debi
    Nancarrow
Richard and Michelle
    Navarre
Rick and Peggy Naylor
Ronald J. Neely
Danielle D. Nelson
Darrel E. Nelson
Diane Newcom
Mary Ann Nichols
Pamela Nocerino
Susan Noltemeyer
Diane Nowak
Blake Nuccio
Pat Oestereicher
Barbara O'Grady
Barry Oliver
Susan Olson
Alyssa Orndorf
Joshua Orndorf
April Orndorf
Hope Ostheimer
Kate Parke
Nancy Parker

Louise V. Parker
Laura Parramore
Vicki Patterson
Julie Payne
Alisan Payne
Fred P. Payne
Gini Pearson
Marilyn Pearson
Becky Perry
Jim and Karen Perry
Bob and Deanna Person
Jane Peterson
Kim Peterson
Annely Peterson
Mary Sue Petticrew
Eileen I. Pfeifer
Sam Winslow Philben
Dan and Judy Polidori
Todd Posinan
Gene Pret
Vincent Pret
Dino Pret
David Putnam
Larry Putnam
Nancy C. Putnam
Deborah Ramsey
Frank and Nellie Rankin
S.M. Raver
Joannie Regester
Edna F. Reid
Aaron Reite
Carolyn Reite
Warren Rempel
Julie Reusser
Robert Reynouard
    Family
Kendra Rhoades
Edith R. Rhodes
Nancy Rice
Myra Rich
Janet M. Richardson
April Richey
Fran Ridgley
Lisa Rigsby
Janet Riley
Richard R. Rizzo
Randy Robbins
Silas Robbins
Lee Robinson
Gayedine Rodriguez
Martha Rodriguez
Hines and Hazel Rogers
Chip and Julie Rogers
Rich Roppa
Hindi Roseman
Jil Rosentnater

Mary Rotola
J. Cooper Rounds
Ruthann Russell
Pat Rustad
Buff and Mary Lou
    Rutherford
Caitlin M. Saling
David M. Saling
Annette D. Saling
Joe and Corrine Sanchez
Bill Saul
James M. Schlarbaum
Debbie Schmit-Lobis
Darlene B. Scott
Bob Scott
Christine Scrip
T. Scruggs
Paulette Shank
Sara Shankland
Kellie Shannon
Joanne B. Shannon
William D. Sharpe
Melanie Shearer
John Sheehan Family
June Simonton
Jill M. Simpson
Shae Singer
Edwin and Frances Sloan
Sandy Smith
Kellen D. Smith
Ronald D. Smith
Larry Solan
Jackie Spacek
Linda Speer
Michael Speer Family
Barbara M. Spencer
Jan Spomer
Nancy Springer
Gully Stanford
Patty L. Stanley
Lis K. Steere
Linda Stephens
Kasia Stevens
Fran Strange
Deborah C. Strom
Jean Strop
Geri Stutheit
Charla Sullivan
Doris Sutton
Lynn Swain
Steve Swanson
Ace Swerdlove
Mary Taitt
Judy Tate
Wendy Wimbush Taylor
Jim and Cindy Tanner

Lindsay Tanner
Julia Rael Tapia
P.C. Tapper
Judy Tate
Mildred P. Teigler
Jim Thompson
Jack and Bonnie Thorne
Eileen Tomaro
Sandy Torres
Sureva Towler
Beatrice Neff Trautman
Chris Tucker
Leslie Tweed
Luanne Unks
Lois Upper
Martha Vair
Kathy VanArsdale
Barbara Van Hook
Mary Vanier
Suzanne Venino
Susan Villano
Linda Vogel
Lynda S. Vogel
Deborah L. Voss
Kendyll Vresilovic
Harry Ward
Stephen and Genie
    Waters
Helle Watson
Mike Way
Robert Wells
Karen Wherley
Joan Wickman
Mary Jean Wiegel
Rosemary Wilkin
Patti Williams
Mary Williams
LaWanna Wilson
Marj Wilson
Frances Wilson
Bill and Marj Wise
Caroline Witty
Duain Wolfe
E.D. Woodring
Robert and Nancy
    Woodward
Ann-Marie Worthington
Frank R. Young
Anthony and Ann
    Zennaiter
Judy Ziegler
Diane Zieroth

...and to all of the
many AAA Colorado
members who responded
to our survey.

Rocky Mountain Resources

Thank you to the many Colorado chambers of commerce, trade associations, arts and humanities organizations, and government agencies who made this book a true reflection of Colorado at Christmastime. Many people helped with the development of this book. They are available to help you with your planning, and we have listed their organizations below.

ASPEN CHAMBER RESORT ASSOCIATION
328 E. Hyman Avenue
Aspen, CO 81612
(303) 925-1940

ASPEN HIGHLANDS SKIING CORPORATION
1600 Maroon Creek Road
Aspen, CO 81611
(303) 925-5300

ASPEN SKIING COMPANY
P.O. Box 1248
Aspen, CO 81612
(303) 925-1220

BASALT CHAMBER OF COMMERCE—MEDC
105 Midland Avenue
Basalt, CO
(303) 927-4031

BRECKENRIDGE SKI CORPORATION
P.O. Box 1058
Breckenridge, CO 80424
(303) 453-5000

BRECKENRIDGE RESORT CHAMBER
P.O. Box 1909
Breckenridge, CO 80424
(303) 453-2913

CASTLE ROCK CHAMBER OF COMMERCE
420 Jerry Street
Castle Rock, CO 80104
(303) 688-4597

CITY OF AURORA, PARKS AND RECREATION
1470 S. Havana Street
Aurora, CO 80012
(303) 344-1776

CITY AND COUNTY OF DENVER
City & County Building
Room 40
Denver, CO 80202
(303) 640-2261 or 640-3386

CITY OF GREELEY
651 10th Avenue
Greeley, CO 80631
(303) 350-9450

CITY OF LOUISVILLE
749 Main Street
Louisville, CO 80027
(303) 666-8331

COLORADO COMMUNITY CHAMBER OF COMMERCE
0590 Highway 133
Carbondale, CO 81623
(303) 963-1890

COLORADO HOTEL & LODGING ASSOCIATION, INC.
999 18th Street, Suite 1240
Denver, CO 80202
(303) 297-8335

COLORADO SKI COUNTRY USA
1560 Broadway, Suite 1440
Denver, CO 80202
(303) 837-0793

COLORADO SPRINGS CONVENTION & VISITORS BUREAU
104 S. Cascade Avenue, Suite 104
Colorado Springs, CO 80903
(719) 635-7506

COLORADO STATE FOREST SERVICE
Colorado State University
    Campus, Forestry Building
Fort Collins, CO 80523
(303) 491-6303

COLORADO TOURISM BOARD
1625 Broadway, Suite 1700
Denver, CO 80202
(303) 592-5410 or
(800) 433-2656

COPPER MOUNTAIN RESORT
P.O. Box 3001
Copper Mountain, CO 80443
(303) 968-2882

CREEDE-MINERAL COUNTY CHAMBER OF COMMERCE
P.O. Box 580
Creede, CO 81130
(719) 658-2374

DOWNTOWN DENVER PARTNERSHIP, INC.
511 16th Street
Denver, CO 80202
(303) 534-6161

DURANGO AREA CHAMBER RESORT ASSOCIATION
P.O. Box 2587
Durango, CO 81302
(303) 247-0312

GLENWOOD SPRINGS CHAMBER RESORT ASSOCIATION
1102 Grand Avenue
Glenwood Springs, CO 81601
(303) 945-6589

GRAND JUNCTION VISITOR & CONVENTION BUREAU
360 Grand Avenue
Grand Junction, CO 81501
(800) 962-2547

GRAND LAKE AREA CHAMBER OF COMMERCE
P.O. Box 57
Grand Lake, CO 80447
(303) 627-3402

GREATER CRAIG AREA CHAMBER OF COMMERCE
360 E. Victory Way
Craig, CO 81625
(303) 824-5689

GREATER DENVER CHAMBER OF COMMERCE
1445 Market Street
Denver, CO 80202-1729
(303) 534-8500

IDAHO SPRINGS CHAMBER OF COMMERCE
P.O. Box 97
Idaho Springs, CO 80452
(303) 567-4382

KEYSTONE RESORT
P.O. Box 38
Keystone, CO 80435
(303) 468-4123

LAKE CITY CHAMBER OF COMMERCE
P.O. Box 430
Lake City, CO 81235
(303) 944-2527

LAKE DILLON RESORT ASSOCIATION
P.O. Box 446
Dillon, CO 80435
(303) 468-6222

LAMAR CHAMBER OF COMMERCE
P.O. Box 1540
Lamar, CO 81052
(719) 336-9095

LONGMONT DOWNTOWN DEVELOPMENT AUTHORITY
528 Main Street
Longmont, CO 80501
(303) 651-8484

MONTROSE COUNTY CHAMBER OF COMMERCE
550 N. Townsend Avenue
Montrose, CO 81401
(303) 249-5515

OLD TOWN MUSEUM & EMPORIUM
420 S. 14th Street
Burlington, CO 80807
(719) 346-7382

OURAY CHAMBER OF COMMERCE
Ouray, CO 81427
(303) 325-4746

PAGOSA SPRINGS AREA CHAMBER OF COMMERCE
P.O. Box 787
Pagosa Springs, CO 81147
(303) 264-2360

PIKES PEAK ARTS COUNCIL
P.O. Box 1073
Colorado Springs, CO 80901
(719) 685-5178

PUEBLO CHAMBER OF
COMMERCE
P.O. Box 697
Pueblo, CO 81002
(800) 233-3446

RIDGWAY VISITOR CENTER
P.O. Box 500
Ridgway, CO 81432
(303) 626-5868

RIFLE CHAMBER OF
COMMERCE
P.O. Box 809
Rifle, CO 81650
(303) 625-2085

SAN LUIS VALLEY ECONOMIC
DEVELOPMENT COUNCIL
P.O. Box 300
Alamosa, CO 81101
(719) 589-7490

STEAMBOAT SPRINGS
CHAMBER RESORT
ASSOCIATION
P.O. Box 774408
Steamboat Springs, CO 80477
(303) 879-0882

TELLURIDE CHAMBER
RESORT ASSOCIATION
P.O. Box 653
Telluride, CO 81435
(303) 728-3041

TELLURIDE SKI RESORT
P.O. Box 1115
Telluride, CO 81435
(303) 728-7404

TOWN OF ESTES PARK
P.O. Box 1967
Estes Park, CO 80517
(800) 443-7837

TOWN OF FRISCO
P.O. Box 4100
Frisco, CO 80443
(303) 668-5276

TOWN OF PALMER LAKE
P.O. Box 208
Palmer Lake, CO 80133
(719) 481-2975

TRINIDAD/LAS ANIMAS
CHAMBER OF COMMERCE
309 Nevada Avenue
Trinidad, CO 81082
(719) 846-928

U.S. AIR FORCE ACADEMY
Colorado 80840-5000
(719) 472-4050

U.S. DEPARTMENT
OF AGRICULTURE
FOREST SERVICE
ROCKY MOUNTAIN REGION
740 Simms
P.O. Box 25127
Lakewood, CO 80225
(303) 236-9431

VAIL RESORT ASSOCIATION
100 E. Meadow Drive
Vail, CO 81657
(303) 476-1000

VAIL VALLEY FOUNDATION
P.O. Box 309
Vail, CO 81658
(303) 476-9500

VAIL VALLEY TOURISM &
CONVENTION BUREAU
100 E. Meadow Drive
Vail, CO 81657
(800) 525-3875

VAIL ASSOCIATES, INC.
P.O. Box 7
Vail, CO 81658
(303) 949-5750

WEST YUMA COUNTY
CHAMBER OF COMMERCE
P.O. Box 383
Yuma, CO 80759
(303) 848-2704

Arts and Humanities Organizations

ArtReach Festival of Trees, Denver
ARTS Elizabeth
Aspen Historical Society
Aurora Dance Arts
Baca/Bloom House and Pioneer Museum, Trinidad
Beulah Valley Arts Council
Bishop Castle, Rye
Central City Opera House Association, Denver
Colorado Symphony Orchestra, Denver
Colorado Council on Arts and Humanities, Denver
Colorado Ski Museum, Vail
Colorado Ballet, Denver
Columbine Chorale, Steamboat Springs
Cross Orchards Historic Site, Grand Junction
Cultural Arts Council of Estes Park
Denver Public Library FRIENDS Foundation
Denver Botanic Gardens
Denver Center Theatre Company
Denver Museum of Miniatures, Dolls and Toys
Durango Arts Center
El Pueblo Museum, Pueblo
Estes Park Historical Museum
Evergreen Area Council for the Arts
Four Mile Historic Park, Denver
Georgetown Loop Railroad
Grand Lake Arts Council
Grant-Humphreys Mansion, Denver
Gully Homestead House, Aurora
Hamill House, Georgetown

Historic Georgetown, Inc.
Holly Commercial Club
Holyoke Community Arts Council
Keep the Lights Foundation, Denver
Kit Carson County Carousel Association, Stratton
L'Esprit de Noel Christmas Home Tour, Denver
Larimer Square, Denver
Limon Promotions Council
Limon Heritage Society
Longmont Museum
Mile High United Way, Denver
Molly Brown House Museum, Denver
Mountain Madrigal Singers, Steamboat Springs
Museum of Western Colorado, Grand Junction
Old Town Museum, Burlington
Ouray County Museum
Ouray Lodge No. 492, B.P.O.E.
Ryssby Church, Longmont
Sangre de Cristo Arts and Conference Center, Pueblo
Silver Plume Singers
Steamboat Springs Arts Council
Strings in the Mountains, Steamboat Springs
Teller House Museum, Central City
Telluride Council for the Arts and Humanities
The Children's Museum of Denver
The Children's Hospital Foundation, Denver
The Denver Center For The Performing Arts
The Denver Santa Claus Shop, Inc.
Vistas of Time, Loveland
Walsh Art Center, Walsh
Wheeler Opera House, Aspen

Photography

Photography provided by the following:

Affleck, Jack, Vail Associates, Inc., 88 (top right), 89, 96

Ashe, Robert, The Brown Palace, 74 (left)

Bartee, Rob, Keep the Lights Foundation, 82-83

Benson, Joan, Crystal Farm, 31

Brown, Larry, The Stock Broker, 92

C Lazy U Ranch, 52, 93

Cook, James A., The Stock Broker, 41

Downtown Denver Partnership, Inc., James A. Rae, 66-67

Durango & Silverton Narrow Gauge Railroad, Durango Area
  Chamber Resort Assoc., 100 (top)

Fielder, John, 2, 7, 8-9, 10-11, 29, 30, 36, 39 (top), 53, 58, 60,
  84, 86, 91, 102-103, 104, 106, 116-117

Harris, Robert E., St. John's Cathedral Archives, 110

Hubbell, National Western Stock Show & Rodeo, 98, 99

Keystone Resort, 88, 89

Laszlo, Colorado Ballet, 63 (top right)

Litz, Brian, 5, 12, 14, 15, 18, 19, 20, 23, 24, 25, 26, 27, 28, 32,
  35, 39 (small), 42, 45, 46, 51, 55, 57 (all), 63 (singers), 64
  (all), 65 (all), 68, 69 (all), 70 (all), 71, 73, 74 (bottom right),
  75 (top & bottom right), 77, 80 (all), 81 (all), 89 (top 3 &
  bottom) 90, 93 (bottom), 94, 95, 98 (center & right), 101,
  108-109, 111, 112 (all), 113 (all), Back Cover

McNeil, Dan, Denver Center Theatre Company, 63 (left)

Rio Grande Denver-Winter Park Ski Train, 100 (bottom)

Ruhoff, Ron, The Broadmoor, 74 (top left)

Simpich Character Dolls, 56, 59, 112 (bottom), 115

Sizelove, Linda, Redstone Inn, 75 (middle)

United States Air Force Academy, 63 (top left)

Recipe and Menu Index

YES! I wish to support the Colorado Children's Chorale* by ordering additional copies of A COLORADO KIND OF CHRISTMAS.

Please send me:

_____ hardcover copies at $35

_____ softcover copies at $25

ALSO AVAILABLE:
Colorado Children's Chorale audio selections! All proceeds benefit the Chorale.

_____ cassette tape at $9.99

_____ CD at $15.99

❏ Check/Money Order Enclosed (payable to Westcliffe Publishers)

NAME

DAYTIME PHONE NUMBER

STREET ADDRESS

CITY   STATE   ZIP

Bill my   ❏ VISA   ❏ MC

CARD NUMBER   EXP. DATE

SIGNATURE

Books available September 15, 1993; Colorado residents please add 7.3% sales tax. Shipping/handling charges: first item $3.50; each add'l item $1.00.

* A portion of book sales ordered with this form benefits the Colorado Children's Chorale.

WESTCLIFFE PUBLISHERS, P.O. Box 1261, Englewood, CO 80150
Phone 303-935-0900; outside Colorado 800-523-3692; Fax 303-935-0903

YES! I wish to support the Colorado Children's Chorale* by ordering additional copies of A COLORADO KIND OF CHRISTMAS.

Please send me:

_____ hardcover copies at $35

_____ softcover copies at $25

ALSO AVAILABLE:
Colorado Children's Chorale audio selections! All proceeds benefit the Chorale.

_____ cassette tape at $9.99

_____ CD at $15.99

❏ Check/Money Order Enclosed (payable to Westcliffe Publishers)

NAME

DAYTIME PHONE NUMBER

STREET ADDRESS

CITY   STATE   ZIP

Bill my   ❏ VISA   ❏ MC

CARD NUMBER   EXP. DATE

SIGNATURE

Books available September 15, 1993; Colorado residents please add 7.3% sales tax. Shipping/handling charges: first item $3.50; each add'l item $1.00.

* A portion of book sales ordered with this form benefits the Colorado Children's Chorale.

WESTCLIFFE PUBLISHERS, P.O. Box 1261, Englewood, CO 80150
Phone 303-935-0900; outside Colorado 800-523-3692; Fax 303-935-0903

YES! I wish to support the Colorado Children's Chorale* by ordering additional copies of A COLORADO KIND OF CHRISTMAS.

Please send me:

_____ hardcover copies at $35

_____ softcover copies at $25

ALSO AVAILABLE:
Colorado Children's Chorale audio selections! All proceeds benefit the Chorale.

_____ cassette tape at $9.99

_____ CD at $15.99

❏ Check/Money Order Enclosed (payable to Westcliffe Publishers)

NAME

DAYTIME PHONE NUMBER

STREET ADDRESS

CITY   STATE   ZIP

Bill my   ❏ VISA   ❏ MC

CARD NUMBER   EXP. DATE

SIGNATURE

Books available September 15, 1993; Colorado residents please add 7.3% sales tax. Shipping/handling charges: first item $3.50; each add'l item $1.00.

* A portion of book sales ordered with this form benefits the Colorado Children's Chorale.

WESTCLIFFE PUBLISHERS, P.O. Box 1261, Englewood, CO 80150
Phone 303-935-0900; outside Colorado 800-523-3692; Fax 303-935-0903

Return Address

_____

_____

_____

PLACE

STAMP

HERE

Westcliffe Publishers

Post Office Box 1261

Englewood, CO 80150-1261

Return Address

_____

_____

_____

PLACE

STAMP

HERE

Westcliffe Publishers

Post Office Box 1261

Englewood, CO 80150-1261

Return Address

_____

_____

_____

PLACE

STAMP

HERE

Westcliffe Publishers

Post Office Box 1261

Englewood, CO 80150-1261